Copyright © 2021
Published and distributed in the United States

All rights reserved. This book or any portion thereof may not be
reproduced or used in any manner whatsoever without the express
written permission of the publisher except for the use of brief quotations
in a book review.

ISBN: 978-1-7363649-6-3
Printed in the United States of America

THORNS IN HER Crown

(A testament to learning how to trust and follow your intuitive process.)

written by:

Erica Brown

Contents

01	Preface	1
02	Have you seen HER?	5
03	Be Dope	15
04	The Differentiating Factor	24
05	Heartbreak is a B_____	33
06	Wait, he said WHAT......?	40
07	Options	47
08	That's all Magic	53
09	Paid in Full	59
10	Beauty in the Struggle	65
11	Marathon Runner	72
12	New Levels, New (Social) Devils	78
13	The Myth v. The Reality of the Strong Black Woman	87
14	The Power of the Twin Necessities	96
15	Life Unapologetically	102
16	Who's Your Connect?	109

Acknowledgements

I started on my journey of telling the story between these pages on September 17, 2017, with no clear blueprint for exactly what I wanted to express and no clear vision of what it would ultimately look like. I didn't know if I was simply journaling my experiences as a way to purge my heart and mind from what I was experiencing at that time or if I'd actually be able to put my words to use by compiling a real in-depth first-person perspective of the constant trials and tribulations I have faced along with many other Black Woman in today's society.

As black women, we are often referred to as queens, in line with the Great Queens of Africa: an ode or message of homage to the likes of Queen Nefertiti. In Biblical history, a thorn of crowns was placed upon Jesus' head during his crucifixion as a symbolic representation by his captors to cause him pain and mock his prophesized authority. The same symbolism is fitting for the title of this book. The heart of a woman belongs to those who nurture from a place of love that runs deeper than the natural eye can see. As self-professed queens, we are often immortalized in color, wearing crowns upon our heads, yet we don't show the thorns that cause us insurmountable suffering. No one pays attention to the thorns within those crowns embedded deep within us. The crown serves as a representation of the expectations placed upon heads by society. Wearing aesthetically beautiful adornments, yet heavy and burdensome, many of us are left with horrendous scars. Still, we continue walking, balancing ourselves upright, refusing to allow anyone to see us tumble, stumble or fall.

This book is my acknowledgment of the scars that we women carry. The scars we attempt to hide while navigating, oftentimes haphazardly, through the turbulent maze of life. This is my attempt to pull back the bandage and expose the gaping wounds we cover with our beautiful headdresses. I want to provide ways to acknowledge and heal those wounds as I recount those life experiences that have provided immense healing to me. If there is anything I can attribute to the healing of another woman, I'd give my last breath to ensure that it happens. We've been covered in pain far too long. For years upon years, we've walked our walks with these beautiful heavy burdens. Now, let's take some time out to talk about what we often carry but rarely expose.

To the Souls who encouraged me along the way.

To the kind entities that propelled me forward when I was unable to move on my own.

To the beautiful, melanin-rich magicians who saved my life by waiting patiently for my stories, giving voice to someone who almost felt she had lost her way far more times than I care to count.

To the Queens below, I simply want to extend a heartfelt THANK YOU...LaKishia Jones, Tiffany Peters, Tiffany Ringer, Cortney Minter, April Streeter, my psychologist & baby sister Elisha McLendon and my Author cousin Ella McLendon. Thank you for covering me when I was unable to cover myself. Thank you for giving me a full-size dose of what I like to call a true "Girl-friend Experience".

To the Kings in my arsenal:

My Father – there are no words to express the how grateful I am for your love over the years. I thank you all for simply being present with me on my journey this lifetime.

Al (Big Tu), Jason Johnson, D. (DJ) Johnson & Donald O. – All excellent representation of Black Men who cover their Queens whether that be a wife, a cousin, friends or neighbors...you show up and I SALUTE you.

To my beautiful boys, my sons, my Future Kings – Aidan and Elijah, all I do is for you, always.

Every word here was written in the name of love, born out of my insatiable desire for growth and the fiery passion burning deep within to heal those around me with my words. God has blessed me with the necessary tools to assist in furthering human development as connected by the veins of sisterhood. Our love for each other must be rooted deeply in spirit and embedded in our souls.

For years, I've walked a large part of my life wishing there was a manual to assist me and show me the way as I attempted to navigate through some of the most challenging situations of my life. I have long searched for something I could relate to. As a disadvantaged black girl from South Side Chicago, I yearned for brutal honesty, unshakable truth, and total transparency in dialogue from those around me who looked like me. I've always had a thirst for knowledge, or what we've come to know as "game".

I've always been intrigued about life's intricacies, wanting to know exactly how things worked and, most importantly, why they work the way that they do. Whatever part of the "game" I could learn, as a willing student of life, I was always front and center. In my effort to pay it forward, I pray that my words resonate in the hearts and minds of those who also thirst for that same knowledge brought forward by us, for us, specifically as women of color. I pray that my words aid in the healing and prosperity of us as a collective. From the streets to the boardroom, many of us so desperately need to know how to maneuver situations to continue to blossom, individually as women and, most importantly, together as sisters. Love, E

Preface

I must open this book by saying if you, my lovely sister, are a woman with the mindset that you need someone by your side to portray a romantic image for the masses, no matter the cost or consequence, then this book may not be for you. If your psyche is hell-bent on perpetuating an image rooted deeply in your own overwhelming need for validation by projecting a perceived idea of happiness – genuine or not – just so you can add Snapchat dinner pics with elongated heart shaped emoji's along with the hashtag #relationshipgoals, then this book, my sister, may not be a suitable read for you.

If this is your line of thinking, and you are content with it, the best thing you can do is tap the beautiful queen sitting next to you and pass this book along. I'm not here to judge you if this is indeed the case. I simply want to save you time, energy, and a world of confusion by asking you to subscribe to a set of ideas that are totally the opposite of your own and maybe even beyond your comprehension. However, if you are not content, it is no coincidence that you are reading this book right now at this very moment. My only goal is for every woman to be happy, more content and at peace with whatever path she chooses for her life. I am not the judge, jury, and executioner here. I am more concerned with tapping into the hearts and minds of those women who walk this earth daily feeling like they are somehow wrapped up in an extremely long episode of a parody for the 'Gram, constantly looking over their shoulders, waiting for the cameras to rush toward them while someone screams, "Gotcha!"

Or those sisters who continually second-guess themselves when those intuitive, God-given spidey senses start tingling in an attempt to steer us away from impending catastrophic doom when they've crossed paths and are now standing face to face with "Mr. Fuck Yo' Life up." I shiver at this thought. It's a scary one, isn't it?

I wrote this book for the young queen who lives her life stuck in perpetual victim mode. You know the ones who are so insulated behind the disguise of a victim mentality that everyone else is the problem; it's never them. Well, this is the group I am speaking to. This book was written for those who carry the burden of low self-esteem partly due to our own self-imposed yet insatiable need to conform to society's measuring stick of who and what you are as a black woman. Or where you should be, positionally, in YOUR life at this very point.

This is for the sistas who wade around in the shallow end of the self-esteem pool, still reeling from the last encounter with an oh so familiar jackass masquerading as a suitable suitor. I write for women looking to build an equal and equitable partnership across every single area of their lives - those of us who have been physically, verbally and/or mentally abused in an effort to diminish our natural God-given light. Those of us who know they're destined for greatness but might have gotten detoured somewhere along the way.

I am specifically carving out this demographic of women because for the longest time, I literally walked this earth feeling like I was in a waking dream. I spent a lot of time wondering, "What the hell is wrong with me?" only to discover later in my journey that nothing is "wrong" with me. It was that nagging sense that something was wrong with me that I spent my whole life trying to solve an imaginary problem. This line of thinking, along with past traumas suffered during childhood, led me from one dead end ass relationship after another for years. I didn't begin to transcend this form of thinking until I started avidly taking notes and subscribed myself to a seven-year bid in the School of Hard Knocks. I literally became a student of life, so to speak. I had to stop thinking that I knew everything. I had to tear down the perception of myself I'd formulated over the years thinking that "I'm wrong" and that I have to fix these flaws in order to obtain what all the other women had in life.

I am a living testament that a skewed perception of your SELF will set you up for a life full of smoke-and-mirror ideas about how life should be and what you should be doing. To that I say, do what brings you joy, happiness, contentment, a sense of accomplishment and peace but not at the expense of sacrificing one for the other. Please note, I am not saying that life should be sought out under the pretense that everything is all sunshine and rainbows with no struggle. I will never tell anyone to pursue rainbows, cotton candy and unicorn dreams, unless that's what you want. However, all things will not always be positive emotional experiences.

My stance here is that we should pursue those things that bring us joy, happiness, contentment, a sense of accomplishment and peace on a level that is relative to each of us individually. What I am telling you is, you don't have to give up either one in an attempt to have them all. Shocking revelation, isn't it? But, Sis, it is so true. Within these pages, I will provide detailed instructions on how to master the art of letting go and simply letting IT (whatever it may be) happen. "It" being the five things I just listed above that we so diligently chase but often cause more harm to ourselves within the process.

This book is a guide to circumvent those pitfalls by providing you with the encouragement, motivation, witty insight, reassurance and confirmation you need to run circles around all the negative things that may come forth to destroy your spirit and completely kill your vibe by hindering you from becoming the BOMB ass woman you are destined to be!

That being said, if you have not stopped reading thus far, and you're still hanging in there with me, turn the page, Sis; we have some real shit to discuss.

Have You Seen Her

2

Well, have you? This is one of those questions I'd like you to ask yourself in the mirror. Have you seen her? Most importantly, do you know who "she" really is?

If you have answered yes, please stop right there. Are you being honest with the proclamation of saying, yes, to knowing who you truly are at this time in your life? Let me be clear, I'm not talking about the glossed over version you present to the physical world and social media on a daily basis. I don't need to know dat BITCH per se. I see her all the time. I see her everywhere. I liken it to walking the streets surrounded by the agents from the Matrix movie: every single one of them look the same.

I'm not seeking the glossy chick when I ask the question, "Have you seen her?" I'm looking for looking for the real you! I don't want to talk to Deja, I'm looking for Dae Dae. I'm waiting for Baby Tee to step up to the plate; you can leave Tameka at the door. If you've seen Candy, send her my way. Candace can politely wait outside, and you can let her know that we'll be done in a few. Because today, Erica didn't show up for this conversation we're about to have, and you are about to get "Rica" (as my mama would affectionately call me). You're getting my alter ego, full and upfront in all her perfectly imperfect glory.

See, Rica is the one who's been hiding herself away from the world. So, as long as I've committed to show up in full, I'd like to have the same commitment from you as we journey through these chapters. I'll wait, Sis. I'll give you a moment to retrieve HER because there's a whole discussion that needs to be had, so let HER know it's safe to come out, and I promise this process this won't hurt the least bit. Trust me, Sis.

Now that I have the attention of the person I need to speak to, I'll start this by asking you why is she hidden in the first place? I know for myself, hiding that imperfectly flawed, emotionally fragile, unsure of herself, confused little girl was a direct result of internalizing years of pain and abuse. The mental trauma that ensued from years of hiding my true unhealed self from the world was almost catastrophic.

I struggled to make sense of the root causes that laid the early foundational groundwork. What was it exactly that lead me to this mountain of uncertainty and self-doubt, which in turn spawned my idea to create a mask, an alter ego so to speak, just to be able to function as semi- normal in my day-to-day life?

The mask I wore day-to-day was a more refined version of who I truly was underneath. My alter ego was this glossed over yet tough as nails persona I created in an effort to shield "her" (my inner damaged little girl) from the piercing eyes of a judgmental society. The mask itself doubled as my defense mechanism and, ultimately, became my own mental prison. For as long as I can remember, I have felt like I had to protect "her" from the often monstrous nature and negative creatures who roam freely among this world we live in.

As we all know, the world – in all its standardized beliefs – is often unkind in its tolerance for perceived mental and psychological abnormalities. I hid myself out of fear that no one would understand the true "her" inside of me. Hell, there were times when I didn't even understand myself, but my fear was that people would continue to cause irreparable harm to my mind, body, and soul if I exposed my true self.

The only way I knew to circumvent the idea of not being accepted, damaged mentally or abused physically was to create a different side of me that I would allow the world to see. If you have indeed brought HER to the table as I've asked, I know you can relate to where I'm going as I attempt to break down the mask/alter egos that so many of us continue to wear.

If you think you're hiding, Sis, I want you to know ... I see you. One thing I am immensely grateful for is my intuitive nature. I can sense pain, insecurity, uncertainty, depression, and low self-esteem from a mile away. It's almost as if I feel it in my soul whenever I encounter another being who's also playing the hiding game, just as I did for so many years. If you're ready to lift that shade and let in the healing light of true self-discovery, I'm here to tell you that you are not alone. In this very moment, it's okay to be yourself in totality. This, my friend, is how we begin our healing journey.

For years, I tucked away the imperfect version of myself and dealt with all her shortcomings, disappointments, mental confusion, and pain... internally. From firsthand experience, I can tell you some of the potential outcomes of choosing to internalize your pain and hide that part of yourself. For one, I became a functionally depressed alcoholic who would occasionally have severe moments of depression that I dealt with on the floor of my master bedroom closet, complete with a bottle of Crown Royal, headphones, and trap music.

Soon enough, the mental paradox of attempting to hide away from the world while pushing forward behind a false persona became my everyday routine. As a result, I found myself drinking alcohol EVERY SINGLE DAY. Drinking was another failed effort to numb the pain I felt when I finally came home to my own four walls - when I finally dropped the masked version of myself, exposing the deep hurt going on inside of my true self.

I kid you not, drinking away my pain became synonymous with Monday, Tuesday, Wednesday, Thursday, Friday, Saturday, and twice on Sunday. Meanwhile, to the outside world I held up an appearance known for slaying dragons during the day all while seamlessly balancing my corporate job, being a single mommy, and continuing to further my education. At night, I'd come home and play supermom to my two wonderful sons, preparing dinner and simultaneously helping with homework. Afterward came the task of getting them ready for bed and ensuring their emotional needs were met for the day while inside I secretly longed for the wee hours of the night when I could retreat to my bedroom closet and continue my self-destructive behavior in peace.

The entire time, I was out here being the "Fearless, Strong-minded, world-conquering Queen" society tells us we need to be. The whole time, I was suffering like hell inside. Can you see the correlation, Erica (by day) versus Rica (by night)? Rica was a very tired, lost, confused soul who had managed to carry and bury the burdens that Erica so willingly picked up during the day. This was my routine, day in and day out.

It was there, alone with my Crown and my trap- in my secret closet space that I realized I actually HATED my job. Yes, I was making good money, especially coming from where I'm from – a product of the hood, a little girl growing up in the struggle known as South Side Chicago. Deep Inside, I came to the realization that I hated the corporate "good ole' boys club" that I'd spent years so desperately trying to penetrate in my quest for self-validation. I wanted to be that sista in control of her own destiny, that bad BOSS ass bitch who'd managed to shatter the glass ceilings in her life. There were more days than not I'd leave work extremely overworked, highly overwhelmed and completely unfulfilled. I fell into the monotony of that same daily routine with the comfort and stability of a guaranteed paycheck as my safety net. There came a point where I had to ask myself the question that I'm sure you've probably pondered at some point in your own adulthood: For what, though? That was the million-dollar probing question! What was I doing this for? What was my divine reasoning for the over-exertion and exhausting pursuit of someone else's structured ideal? I had to ask myself this question, and, most importantly, I had to be HONEST with myself. Don't get me wrong, I've always been somewhat of a hustler. I grew up on Chicago's South Side, in one of the most infamous neighborhoods, known as Englewood. I mean this chick (me of course) lived her ENTIRE life in full defense mode, do you hear me?

I have been playing defense so long that I can usually predict a move long before it even happens. If you managed to survive growing up in impoverished urban America, you know exactly what I mean. I had very little adult oversight from the age of 14 into adulthood. Some of my most valuable life decisions were made in the clutch, so to speak. I had to think fast and react even faster, and if that reaction required me to take a blow to the chest, I had to brace myself for impact. Even as I took those hits my only objective was to get back up even quicker than I'd fell. I know that so many who are reading this can relate. Like I said, I have ability to see far beyond the so-called "representative".

Fast forward a few years into womanhood, what did I do with all that I'd learned growing up in the concrete jungle? Who did I become when I was faced with a sink or swim ultimatum on a regular basis? To put it short, I became a victim in hiding. You know that seemingly innate thing that happens to most of us when we're handed an oversized Louie Vuitton bag of repeated losses. Or, how about when you take on traumatizing situation after traumatizing situation without taking the time to properly dissect, learn and – most importantly – **GROW** from those same traumatic experiences?

Many of us simply become masters of the masquerade. We create what we portray as a separate entity that we ultimately present to the world, every day somewhere between the hours of, let's say, 6:00am to 6:00pm. But baby, when that curtain comes down and that persona becomes a lonely pit of emptiness from which SHE (that little girl you've been hiding) longs to escape and breathe in new life and light even if only for a moment.

This is where many of us are conflicted. Because see, we've been taught to pull ourselves up by our bootstraps and keep it moving no matter the trial. We never truly deal with the pain. Never deal with those deep-rooted feelings of inadequacy. Never deal with the idea that YOU don't know it all and the realization that YOU don't have it all together. You don't! I am here to tell you, Sis, there is nothing wrong with any of those realizations.

Let those masks down! Your inner little girl deserves to smell the fresh air. Dig deep and let her out sometimes. You'll be surprised how fresh air and an evolved perspective renews the soul. By the way, the day of reckoning I speak of above happens to a large percentage of us women at some point in our respective journey.

You will one day wonder, why? You will one day question your journey and if that roadmap is truly leading you to where YOU (barring societal influences) truly want to go. Believe it or not, I am still learning it to this very day! I have decided to subscribe to life-long studentship. Trust me when I say, you are never too old or too together in your life to learn something new whether it be new habits, a new mindset or set new benchmarks in your life.

Your personal healing is the most important thing you will ever accomplish, and my goal is to help us break the stigma of having to be who and what others assume we should be. You don't have to fit in anyone's BOX! Besides, it's always best to create your own packaging, love.

I want you to know that you do not have to suffer in silence any longer, Sis. You don't have to continue playing hide-and-seek with yourself. This is my call to roll up your sleeves and get prepared to really get in there and do the hard work necessary to permanently alleviate your mask-wearing days.

You must actively work on revealing, acknowledging, restoring, and healing those parts of YOU you've been conditioned to tuck away from the world. The world needs you in complete totality! To give away only fragmented pieces when 100% of you is absolutely required to accomplish your own personal goals and achieve your desires. To show up in pieces is not only short-changing yourself but also the world that awaits your unique contributions! To show up shattered further highlights the point that you are not at PEACE with yourself when you continue to show up in pieces.

We give away pieces when we're not at peace within. When we are incapable of giving ourselves fully, we divide our output which can ultimately lead to severe mental and emotional conflict. Your true self is out of alignment. This is where severe burnout is born and bred, Sis! Get out before you burn out. Make the commitment to cultivate a better, WHOLE you. A whole you who shows up fully aware, fully able, and fully capable of serving your life's mission, whatever that may be for you.

Here's another way to look at it, love: you're grown, and NO ONE, and I do mean no one, is going to beat your ass for the decisions you make at this point in the game. Decide to choose YOU! Choose your healing. Choose your path. You have the right to say I'm not okay but if you give me some time, I promise you I will be.

Now, I'm not telling you to throw caution to the wind when it comes to wellbeing of self and the wellbeing of those who rely or depend on you, i.e., your children. I'm simply saying that no one can tell you who YOU need to be! You have to forge that path on your own, wholly and solely. Even the words I am writing to you today cannot paint your narrative. You are the author of your own story. My attempt is to get you two (the hidden you and the newly emerging you) on the same page. I am speaking from direct experience. My words come from a place of love and concern.

There was a point in my life when I was exactly where you are now. I, too, suffered in silence while attempting to balance that role-playing act that so many of us take on. I know for a fact that I am a very smart woman. I am often a ferocious force to be reckoned with. I am also relentless when it comes to pursuing my goals. I can hold my weight with the best of them, from the streets to the boardroom. I will never allow anyone to tell me, "NO, you can't have it." I don't need your permission to get it, I am simply going to take it! That's how I roll.

However, the damaged hidden little girl in me spent years marred in the shadows, struggling with self-doubt, self-loathing, feeling unappreciated and unprotected. I struggled greatly with moments of insecurity. I've wrestled with bouts of extreme anger and severe depression. I've also struggled with addiction while trying to fit my oversized ass into the societal mold. The same mold that no matter how hard I tried I always managed to feel like I didn't really belong. Why? Because I was perpetrating. I wasn't showing up in complete oneness. I was masking and hiding, just trying to fake my way along.

Now, as I approach 40 years old, I am literally amazed at people's reaction when I express my truth about that damaged little girl I used to hide deep within. I often get reactions of pure shock because that's not who I allowed the world to see. For a long time, I didn't give HER (the hidden me) the care she needed to heal and the opportunity become fully integrated with new (emerging) me, the truly fearless one.

While I won't confess to having a full blown large-scale identity crisis, there were some identity conflicts when it came to the person I felt I was at my core versus who I allowed the world to see. I don't need to have a Ph.D. in human behavioral psychology to know that hundreds upon thousands of us (women) carry a similar burden and are left to deal with some of the same issues I faced.

If you can relate, Sis, please know that you are blessed beyond measure to already have enough self-awareness to acknowledge the part of you that needs major work! I always say the best gift a child could receive is a strong sense of who they are, as early as possible in life.

The sooner we are in tune with who we are now the more aware we are as we evolve over time and encounter new life lessons, engaging in different experiences. If you know who you are now, who you've locked away in the past and the version of you that you desire to be, the sooner you can marry them and come out as a whole functional, thriving human being. The time is upon us now to set you free and step fully into the new you! It's time to get reacquainted and re-acclimated, SIS…. Let's do this!

Be Dope   3

Label me a BOSS! Yeah, I said it. I am the Boss of my destiny and fulfiller of my dreams. As the steward of my overall well-being, I am in charge of cultivating and maintaining my own happiness. As the sole keeper of my own self fulfilment, I began to implement measures in my life that pushed me to zero in on the core root of what I needed in my life not only to attain happiness but also provided me the tools to maintain my own individual state of happiness.

So, I tasked myself with the duty of carving out ideas in my mind that I deemed to be tangible and attainable goals for myself. This task required me to move beyond the goal itself and pinpoint the contributions I would be willing to make towards attaining them. Sis, I don't give a damn if your dream is to sell peaches under the interstate overpass. Whatever you desire, born of your own God-given talents, walk forward in your gifts boldly and be the very best at it! I am a strong believer that we are all born with a uniquely identifiable set of skills that make us who we are: that one-of-a-kind thing that aids you in pursuing your passions with determination and fervor. Use that "thing" as your "sorry not sorry" pass as you maneuver through life, attempting to shake the weight of society and all of its implied restrictions.

If you're not living for you, then who are you living for? That's a really great question! I've had to go back and ask myself this question numerous times over the course of my life. I don't know if you've ever encountered people who are so great at telling you exactly what YOU should be doing or how YOU should be doing it, yet they have never managed to build anything of substance for themselves.

We've all had encounters with people who swear they can live our lives better than we ever could. Even with that said I'm going to stop here and ask, what is your motivation for reading my book? I surely hope the answer is not so I can tell you what to do with your life, because I could never tell you explicitly what it is you need to do to find contentment in your heart. I can't give you a play by play, step by step account of what drives you. I can only help you explore your inner self and discover those driving forces necessary to contribute to your own wellbeing. I can also tell you from experience that you will continually spin your wheels, trying to live out somebody else's script. You need to become your own author, baby! You have to walk forward boldly in your own endeavors, penning the tale of your own story. And you must be totally unapologetic while doing so.

Do you know how many successful people were told what they couldn't do? Do you know how many self-made entrepreneurs before you were told that their ideas weren't formidable or scalable business ventures? Do you know how many financially prosperous individuals were told why their paths to fulfillment wouldn't work? Trust me, there have been many! However, let me ask you this: how many people have had your heart, your vision, your drive, your passion and your desire to cultivate what specifically brings you JOY?

Ooh, I know that answer! The answer is, NONE. You are the painter, your vision is your paintbrush, and the world is your canvas. See, society teaches us to color within the lines and follow the systematic path of life we're all groomed to adapt to as children. Think about it, Sis. You go to school to pick a career. From the career choice you are taught how to be proficient and knowledgeable to perform that specific career function. Then you go out into the world after all those years of formal training and work that career path until you can successfully retire.

Now, I'm not saying there is anything wrong with this outline. I'm simply saying this outline does not always account for this thing called, real muthafuckin' life! We spend our younger years scratching and clawing at the top spot. Meanwhile, we rack up all kinds of bullshit ass baggage as we are overworked, underpaid, stressed the hell out and stretched too damn thin for the remainder of our career duration.

Then one day we have this grand epiphany: this model cannot be all there is to life. This revelation hit me in my mid 30's and I'm almost 100% positive you have pondered the same as well. This is where we must learn to treat those driving forces toward our personal happiness as if they were monetary contributions and deposit them into our personal wellbeing bank! Our investment to build a self-sustaining reservoir will also yield a way to cash in on your own unique DOPENESS. Leverage your investments towards pursing your passions diligently. Nothing will yield a better dividend then being at peace in your pursuit of building a better quality of life for yourself.

Believe it or not, it took me nine years to start writing this book. After three years of false starts and failed personal deadlines – and there were many – I finally committed to my goals the same way I commit to my 9 to 5. I swear to you, I have enough written material to publish ten books if I wanted to at this point. All I needed was enough gasoline to ignite my fire. That came in the form of a completely stalled career, financial instability, and a failed engagement. It was only then that I decided I wanted to level up in every aspect of my life but this time I had to do it on my own terms with my own damn roadmap.

It took for this perfect trifecta of issues to truly light a fire in me; to not only talk about it but take the necessary steps to be about it. I watched myself pour my feelings onto blank pages over and over again in my best effort to share my experiences, with the intention of helping to heal those who looked like me. And I knew the struggles I'd faced weren't much different from the average woman who has been subject to the same issues in life. On the other hand, as a form of self-sabotage I became so discouraged and obsessed with the idea that no one actually cared what I had to say that I would trash each project I started. I'd save multiple drafts of my work to my laptop and move on with my mediocre ass life. It was as if I was terrified of greatness. I was completely afraid to bank on me, to bank on E!

My fear was rooted in the fact that I am solely responsible for the failure of my vision. But what I'd failed to remember is that I am also equally responsible for any successes associated with my vision as well. In my heart of hearts, I knew with 100% certainty that I'd lived a very interesting life thus far – a life filled with some pretty traumatic experiences. A life wrought with mind and soul altering consequences designed to kill, steal, and destroy the soul of most people.

Yet I made it through each one, just as I'm sure you have if you're reading this. And to this very day, I am super grateful that I am no longer a victim of the circumstances I've endured. Instead, I emerged from every one of those fires, and have been refined by them and renewed in my womanhood. I am now an ever-evolving victor! Each experience we go through is designed to bring us out on the other side a little bit wiser and a helluva lot stronger than we were before.

Bosses take losses too! If anyone tells you differently then I'd say they aren't in tune enough with their true inner self, the part that allows for honest self-reflection and opens us up to being accountable and transparent about our own shit. Revealing that extra layer of transparency is something many of us women so vitally need today. Some will appear to favor the "smoke and mirrors" route when it comes to being true to themselves and vocalizing their past struggles.

That's fine; whatever gets them through. However, I don't' subscribe to the red pill philosophy, Sis. Blue pill me all day long. I like my truth just like my drinks straight – no chaser. I am here to tell anyone who will listen that losses are the seeds planted in the budding stage of every necessary lesson in life. The beauty is in recognizing the lesson while your bruises are just scabbing over and still healing from one of life's proverbial beat downs.

To think I spent so many years wrestling with the validity of what I had to say in my writings. I questioned how my story and my lessons on this journey would be perceived. Hell, I struggled with the notion of no one really giving a damn about what I have to say with the exception of my close friends who, of course, will support me no matter what.

On the other side of that coin, one thing I knew deep within the core of my soul is that writing was as essential to me as air. I have often told others that I literally see words in my head just like you see colors on an artist's palette. Words give life to the unspoken parts that so desperately long to be heard. I've known and felt this in my soul my entire life. As sure as the sun rises in the sky, writing, for me – specifically painting vivid stories with unique wordplay – was my God-given talent. I was given a story to share. A story to heal. My duty has always been to tell my story, to write and put it out into the world for those who have found themselves in a similar situation to know that they are not alone.

However, knowing this and bringing to life all the ideas I held inside were two totally different things. I didn't trust my vision. Therefore, I spent years evading my own dopeness. That's what it is, by the way: your glory in your story is what makes you dope. Our stories are the breadcrumbs we leave for those who come up behind us. If I can lessen the hard knock blow that life will surely hand out for another young girl coming up behind me, why would I continue to sit on my dreams?

I encourage every single one of you to dream as big as your being will allow. Hell, I even say push beyond those boundaries and cultivate your dreams in such a way that they have no choice but to continually expand outward into the infinite spaces of the Universe.

There are absolutely no limits! The only limitations are the ones we accept and impose upon ourselves, and the limiting beliefs we choose to believe.

These are the only barriers along your path to greatness. I implore you not to focus on what you've convinced yourself you can't do by focusing on the things you can readily accomplish at this very moment. This process is what I call taking the "Baby Steps" method to undo those self-imposed restrictions. I can tell you with absolute certainty that the proof is the pudding!

Here's an example. Think back to a time when there was something you really wanted to have or accomplish. I mean that thing you went to sleep envisioning in your dreams and woke up with it pulsating through your veins the next morning. We've all had that "thing" we wanted so badly that everything we did began to circle around obtaining it - like vultures circling a fresh carcass. For me, there was a time in my life when all I wanted to do was crack $75,000 a year in annual salary built solely on my ability to hustle and the idea of leveraging my strong work ethic as a vessel to get me there.

Honestly, in my eyes, I didn't have much else I could use. I'd dibbled and dabbled in and out of college for years. I'd grown up in an environment where the idea of going to college was simply a far-fetched pipe dream. So, I learned early on how to hustle my way through corporate America. I taught myself every single MS Office program used in the modern office environment. I'd land a job, find out who the star player was and link up with them to position myself where I could effectively learn everything they knew. Then, I'd consistently take the new things I learned and apply them without instruction from anyone. I learned early that the best route is taking the proactive approach. As I moved through different points in my career, racking up different skillsets and branding myself as that person who will do what no one else is willing to do, I became an employee of value.

I recruited professional mentors to assist me along the way. I linked myself with others who were further along in their careers than I was at the time. I took the time to study their movements, ask the right career questions, and develop my own strategies based on their feedback. I became obsessed with that dollar amount and reaching that point before a certain age.

Well, I can say that I accomplished that goal some time ago by focusing on what I wanted and stopping at nothing until the dream became a reality. There is nothing wrong with having a healthy obsession of obtaining the things in this life you want for yourself. This is the fuel to your fire, Sis. A dream will lay out its own roadmap; all you have to do is push forth and follow through.

I can almost hear it now, "What does this have to do with being a boss?" The idea of what makes a person a "Boss" is subjective. So, I say ,pursue whatever fulfills your purpose, funneled by your passion. If working for someone else is more your agenda, then there is no static from me Sis! However, I'd encourage everyone to take an active ownership stake in something you can build for yourself to one day operate as sole owner and proprietor.

Exercise 1.0

Imagine someone told you today that you only had 6 months left to live and the conditions in which you will live out those next 6 months are dependent on the environment you create for yourself. Equipped with a definite date of expiration, name 3 things you would choose to diligently pursue to create the best 6 months of your remaining life. Take your time and thoroughly consider this scenario then provide your list below.

1. _____

2. _____

3. _____

Looking at the list you've provided above, answer this, "What's stopping you from bringing these things to fruition right now at this very moment?"

The Differentiating Factor... 4

I always say it takes a survivor to recognize a victim on sight. I don't care what disguise we attempt to wear to conceal our inner pain; believe it or not – in some way, shape, form, or fashion – it shows. On the flip side, you must be aware that a predator can also smell the blood of its prey from a mile away. You must know that if you're perusing through life leaking blood, no matter how much eyeshadow, MAC foundation, and lipstick you pack on, you're only fooling the person in the mirror.

Listen, it does not matter how many pairs of Louboutins you stack in your closet or Gucci handbags you sling, there is always a parasitic predator who will eventually pick up the scent from that seemingly invisible trail of blood you've left behind. Without properly addressing and treating those past traumas, you're basically handing over every secret ingredient needed to feed the appetite of said predator.

As me and my girls would say, "Mr. Fuck Your Life Up" will find an angle to get you. Trust me when I say that he (or she) will find you. This person doesn't even have to be a love interest. It can be a friend, a colleague, or even a relative. All they need is the space and opportunity to get a nice whiff of your damaged scent.

Before you know it, you've been scoped out, scooped up, and in the grasp of a full on spiritual, physical and/or mental attack. Knowing there are people in this world who will mercilessly and maliciously prey on your pain, it is key that you're ready and well-prepared. Especially as we grow older in our life's journey, the goal is to evolve, focusing primarily on healing the scars we carry. Everything we do should project as a testament to heal, not an invitation to hell. Chaos and turmoil are right around the corner; there is no need to call it to you. Don't treat the gaping wounds of your past and it'll find you like a wolf on fresh meat.

For many years, I thought only I knew that damaged little girl kept hidden deep in my personal space of solitude. I thought she was my best kept secret. Yet, I've run across many men who spotted my brokenness on sight. Most of them were as equally hurt as I was, yet they somehow managed to get a good glimpse of my little secret. As much as I thought I'd kept hidden, it turns out my pain wasn't as hidden as I'd assumed, and nine times of out ten, I'd already welcomed in my adversary before I'd even become aware of their mission.

I was so exposed, yet I was the only one unaware of that fact. A true predator will know the perfect time to strike; as soon as your rawest parts are on full display they go in for the kill. Once the enemy has spotted the weakness of his/her opponent, there is pretty much nothing you can do besides lace up your Nike's and prepare for the impromptu track session because they are going to run you, Sis!

Dragging season will certainly be in full effect. And by the time you finally come to terms with the fact that your perceived

King T'Challa has now become the Terminator of all things positive and peaceful in your life, it's likely you are already at a detrimental disadvantage. Imagine stepping into the boxing ring with no gloves for a full sparring match with Satan himself. Although my description is a bit dramatic, don't discount how far a beat down of the mind, body and soul can take you. Some of us never make it back from these matches. So, what do you do, Sis? It's so easy to look up and find yourself fully engaged with what you thought was your Knight in shining armor, only to find an unevolved monster lurking patiently just beneath a quiet freshly polished surface. It is critical to deal with those wounds before you offer yourself to the world. You have no idea what's out there. Most importantly, you have no idea who or what your scent is inviting in.

How do we address our past wounds?

TRY THERAPY HUN, I DID and STILL DO!

Before you offer your scars to the masses, try talking to a trained professional if you simply aren't equipped with the internal tools needed to stitch yourself up! The goal is to end the perpetual cycle of victimhood. Can you honestly say that you're a "victim" if you willing to stick your hand into a lion's cage waving a raw freshly cut steak?

The answer is emphatically NO. You knew the risk, yet you took a chance. If you won't say it, I will! Now that things aren't in your favor, you have to deal with those consequences. Take that L, feel it... embrace it... learn from it and move forward love! You can also try using your close inner circle to aid you in the healing process. My close girlfriends and I have weekly, if not daily, pow-wow sessions to simply discuss life from the respective eyes of 30-something-year-old women who have LIVED and, most importantly, learned. We all try to exercise putting forth the conscious effort required not only to learn but also to grow from our previous missteps. We've made a pledge of allegiance to a United Peace of Mind built by self-preservation, self-appreciation, and liberation of societal pressures, for ALL.

Seriously, as a collective, my girlfriends and I have pledged to remain life-long students of the game. I must say, my friends are some of the most HONEST and amazingly transparent people I know. And if you don't have that kind of inner circle, love, get yourself one! It's important to keep people around you who can remove their biased feelings and give the assistance you need to get through with a whole lot of love, a little compassion, and a constant reality check! We genuinely try to hold each other accountable for every ounce of fuckery that occurs on our watch.

Let me clarify, this isn't a social gathering of chicks cackling away, sipping wine (okay, we do sip), complaining about all the overused stereotypes that lead to the ultimate all-bruthas-ain't-shit conception. We rarely spend our time painting victim portraits! Trust when I say that this kind of bitter behavior is NOT our idea of a sip and paint. Personally, I get zero pleasure from painting men, specifically black men, as nothing but low-down dirty dogs. I cannot and will not subscribe to that line of thinking.

I know too many good-hearted, kind-spirited, emotionally stable, communicatively clear-missioned men who are sincerely making dope ass contributions to the world. Instead of bashing, I choose to wholeheartedly SALUTE these bruthas every single chance I get.

I don't think people know how much pride beams in me when I meet men of color who have done the work it takes to heal, grow and evolve into positive contributors to our society. And no, I don't believe that marriage or the ability to maintain a long-standing relationship should be the only measurements of a good man's worth. Again, I look at the core of a person's being. I examine the nature of their heart, the clarity of their thoughts, how their thinking resonates. I admire the pronounced dedication that exudes in the way these Bruthas move, as they continue to fight against the stereotypes and barriers unfairly assigned to them as black men in society. I applaud bruthas who stand in the gap for their families, their community, and the younger ones who come behind them. Sis, you don't have to be involved with these men romantically to deem that stand up brutha a good man. If he's not a viable romantic option for you, does that make him any less a viable candidate for creating change in the world? Does that take away from all the other wonderful contributions I just mentioned?

Ladies, we have to take a cue here! Just because a brutha is not boo'd up with us or willing to become your long-awaited knight in shining armor, don't let that take away from his other beaming qualities. Give our Kings their crowns while they're here. If you know or have a solid man in your life, salute him and know that what's for you is for you! Your King is coming, I promise when you're ready- all things working together in divine harmony will deliver. In the meantime, invest time in getting yourself ready to operate on his frequency. When you stay ready, you never have to get ready. OK!

As much as I love a strong solid ass brutha, I think it's imperative to note that one or two (or ten) bad apples should never ruin the whole bunch for you, Sis. Take a moment to heal from those unevolved creatures you've encountered before. Don't let them ruin your taste for the entire collective of Kings that surround us daily. It's so easy to become addicted to that pill of bitterness.

This I know for sure! I've surely had my moments in which bitterness tried to creep in like a thief in the night. You have to stay on point love and actively work to guard your heart against that wicked bitch of bitterness. Your armor is the work you're willing to invest in healing yourself. See, when you are busy about you, you can't be busy about them... you know what I mean? You're not concerned about harboring resentment or bad feelings toward a man who you feel has done you wrong in the past.

Self-healing is the bitterness antidote. Once we can open ourselves up to initiating our own healing, we put a stick in that perpetual victim wheel, stopping it dead in its tracks. As we grow in our quest to become self-sustaining through personal accountability, we take away the power to be subdued by subpar ass individuals and their subpar ass issues. Being accountable means that we are no longer the women who so willingly profess undying loyalty to the first man who shows up, looking for the "ride or die" bitch.

We can ride, but we cannot continue to kill ourselves mentally and spiritually behind the usual antics that come with the emotional immaturity and unresolved past trauma of our potential suitors. I'll ride, but baby I'm not dying for anyone. The greater question is, why would a person who professes to love me even want me to "die" for their love and affection in return?

This thinking makes absolutely no sense, Sis. A healthy love will protect you from harm, not force you towards it. Can we please stop with our overt willingness to thrust ourselves onto love's sword to prove our worthiness in a relationship? I am here to let you know that it is not, and never has been, your "job" as a woman, a partner, or a wife.

As a matter of fact, looking back over our lineage, I know many of us have those familial matriarchs that set the archetype for these "Ride or Die" type relationships. Your grandmother, as did mine, might have put it all on the line and remained a stoic partner throughout the trials and tribulations of her marriage. These women likely endured long suffering over the course of their lives and marriages for reasons beyond our understanding due to shift in generational times. And to be honest, that's fine, Sis, if you're built that way. However, so many of us are not, which is why we must try to change this sacrificial lamb mentality when it comes to how we engage with our partners.

Why has there always been so much expectation placed on women to bare the brunt of a man's growing pains and subsequent shortcomings? Why are we given the task of sacrificing ourselves so that another may reap the benefit of our unconditional love? I'm putting that idea to rest, Sis, right here within these pages. A healthy love is reciprocal, not a one-sided sacrifice. I want to take a moment to point out the relational paradigm shift that has happened in the last 25-35 years as women have moved away from upholding that sacrificial lamb mentality. Many of us women can easily afford a life filled with certain liberties that were inaccessible to our grandmothers and mothers before us.

We do not have the same pressures to remain silent sufferers within relationships anymore. Today's woman can successfully maneuver in dodging those old-age taboos that kept women in the past tied to unfulfilling relationships. One key contributor: as a society we've managed to take the fear out of divorce. Many of us aren't afraid of being a single mother anymore. And dare I say it, some have mastered the art of being alone – relishing their peace and spiritual rehabilitation until MR (MRS.) Right, comes along.

I will never say anyone should aspire to divorce and/or single parenthood, etc. because – as someone who's walked this path – I can attest to the fact that it is some tough shit to handle! All I'm saying is the main things that we as women once feared have transformed into surmountable hurdles on the track of life. If you're focused enough, and you can keep your momentum going when it's time to jump those hurdles, you'll do so with confidence and perseverance.

It is largely my belief that fear coupled with the climate of affairs, especially for minorities, has shaped many of our grandparents' and parents' marriages. And just because you don't have that "old school" love that the older folks tend to glorify does not mean that there is something oddly wrong with you! Many times, you've just learned to stand a little taller, a little prouder, and a little higher in your standards. Again, nobody knows better than you what you want and, more importantly, the precise things you need to cultivate those spaces of contentment, peace, joy and happiness of your own.

Remember, Sis, we have to get in there and heal those old wounds! This process can ultimately determine the characters and personalities you attract in your life. Not all encounters will harm you, but many are definitely designed to help you grow. Examine the layers of your own personal process, work those layers with the goal of carving out your own monuments of glory. A Life lived vs. Lessons this life has to give, study them both love and know the difference!

"Women who came before you carved out your path ahead. The steps you create on this journey have since made you a GIANT in your right, no longer shrinking in the shadows behind them"
– E. Brown

Heartbreak is a B*&%h   5

That's about as clear cut as it gets: not one lie told here. If you've ever experienced it firsthand then you know that the depths of pain derived from the loss of a relationship, partnership, or friendship can run deep and continue to cut deeper long after the initial blow has passed.

Many of us carry past pain around with us like the newest fall collection designer handbag. We tend to wear our pain as an accessory, dragging it in and out of subsequent relationships, picking up more pieces and moving right along. That's what we were taught to do. Pick up the pieces and keep it moving, right? That mentality seems to be the black woman's creed.

I tell all my people that there are no shortcuts when healing from heartbreak. The only sure fire way I know to successfully recover from heartache is to simply let it happen! Acknowledge your feelings as they arise in the aftermath of a breakup and make it a point to learn from any personal contributions that led to the demise of the relationship. Allow those feelings to occur in that moment but do NOT get stuck there. Although there are stages to heartbreak, it's easy to find yourself still stuck in the initial stage of the breakup, looping the pain over and over on repeat in your mind.

I know, unfortunately, as I've lived each stage of heartbreak, with some stages on incessant replay at different points in my life. These stages usually cycle in feelings of anger, deep sadness, physical pain, lack of appetite, lack of sleep, confusion, anger again (yes, that one tends to linger) and disbelief. Next, the realization of what has occurred tends to become a tad clearer in our vision. Upon realization of said events, the road should begin to lead us into the final stage of acceptance, resulting in some form of closure that, in turn, illuminates a path towards healing. And while it can be nice to have that final curtain call with your ex, you do not need the other party to obtain closure, my dear. No, ma'am, you do not, but we'll save that speech for another book.

When I say that this is a ZERO judgment zone, Sis, I mean it. We've all been to the disgusting pit of heartbreak hell. We emerge from those initial stages of pain to find ourselves stuck in that blank space of heartbreak purgatory. Oftentimes, it feels like I have a permanent rental spot in said purgatory, especially since I vacationed there quite often over the course of my life. But one thing is for sure and two things for certain: the pain will pass!

Have you ever stood on a beach and just observed the tide as it rises and then subsides? It comes rushing in so strong and overpowering, then as the waters begin to settle and recede. The sand beneath is glistening in the sun - even brighter than before. When we're in the midst of it, we are often unable to see the light at the end of the tunnel.

It usually feels like all hope is lost and nothing will ever be right again in the world. In all honesty, I've even managed to overcome those initial feelings as I waded deep in that pain and simply allowed it to happen. I had to feel it in the core of my bones! It is uncomfortable and excruciating when you're in the midst of it. Some will do whatever they can to numb the intensity of the pain by turning to alcohol, drugs, or some other form of self-deprecating behavior.

While I will never condone causing further harm by indulging in these things, I will say that I completely understand why many choose to do so. Being in that painful space is no fucking joke, definitely not for the weak at heart. And, Sis, if you're not strong enough to guide yourself through it, feeling it, acknowledging it, and allowing it to transform you, it is very easy to lose yourself and your sanity in the process.

I know what I'm advising sounds like a total set up, right? Let me tell you, the first time I heard this advice from my dad, I seriously had to question how much he really loved me. How could my own father have the audacity to tell me I needed to sit with all that mental and emotional pain I was feeling at that time? The only thing my psyche could respond with was, "Hell fuckin' no, not happening." How could he be so willing to give such a daunting directive to his own daughter and expect me to follow that advice?

Initially, my willingness to take his advice fell somewhere between an emphatic, "NO" and a sarcastic "Yeah, okay" (insert the ghetto-est of ghetto eye rolls), and I meant this with all of the sarcasm in my little light-skinned soul. I wanted no part of any of that. Listen,

I was convinced he could not possibly love me, giving me that kind of advice. Turns out, the old man knew a thing or two! The first time I stopped fighting all those crushing feelings of despair; you know that feeling in your chest that feels like someone took a pair of pliers and went in to rearrange your upper ribs? The second time I stopped fighting those feelings and just allowed them to happen in total and complete submission was when the healing power began.

When we become fully aware of the pain we're feeling while simultaneously acknowledging it's all-encompassing destructive nature, using it as our transformative vessel, then we can allow the pain to carry us through a cyclonic force while feeling both the darkness and the light of heartbreak. In this moment, we can embrace the amazing transformative power of love within our own suffering.

I was completely blown away by the fact that even through the storms – which I equated to being the worst feelings I could ever possibly feel in life – I swear I felt as if the universe was hugging me and covering me in its soothing essence all at the same time. I liken the feeling and its aftermath to that of a mother who may chastise her child from a place of stern love. Yes, it will temporarily hurt them, but it's designed for their betterment. So, your mission is to boldly step back into this world with a healthy desire to love again, knowing in your heart of hearts that none of what you have experienced is personal! Heartbreak isn't an attack on your person, your individual womanhood, or the fragility of one's heart. It is simply one moment in a lesson designed to push you beyond your current level of understanding. You did in fact pray for the "level up", right?

If you can bring yourself to wrap your mind around the idea that pain is love in a different form, you will see that the two are one and the same. There is no separation here; only how you perceive it! You simply cannot have one without the other. All feelings are temporal – pain, happiness, joy, love, loss, etc. They pass through you in fleeting spurts just like the wind. Personally, I choose to acknowledge all feelings, even those I perceive as negative, like the hurt of heartbreak, and let it float right through me. As for the more positive feelings, I choose to hold on and relish in those feelings just a tad bit longer. This requires making a conscious concentrated effort to hold onto those extra little moments of love's afterlight as it passes through you.

Keep that same energy, Sis. In my experience, you'll start to notice the strength of these negative feelings lessen over time. The positive feelings will begin to have a much bigger and stronger impact. Again, I am not telling you what I heard; I have lived this and overcome heartbreak time and time again.

If I... HER... ME... SHE can overcome some of the most painful shit you could ever imagine, I know for a fact that you got this, babe! Listen, if I delved deeper into the some of the things I've been through, you'd probably need two Xanax, a whole bottle of wine, and a box of Kleenex to make it through this book. Just know that I'm not doing that today. I'll save that for another read. Plus, I honestly don't think you're reading this to indulge in a pity party. Remember, no victims here, we are VICTORS!

Exercise (this helped me greatly).

- Find a quiet place that resonates with your spirit, a place that makes your inner soul smile whenever you are there. For me, it's being outside in nature amid awe-inspiring scenery.
- After you've found that space for you, go sit there and simply allow yourself to BE in the moment!
- In your quietness, pay extra special attention. Be sure to watch the thoughts and feelings as they flow through you during this quiet period. When I say watch, I mean notice it, give it proper acknowledgment, and let it float on!
- In this process, try your best not to assign a specific meaning to those feelings (bad, painful, gut-wrenching or the "I can't believe he/she did this to me…, etc.)

As you begin to practice this as often as you can, you'll also begin to notice your indifference towards each feeling that passes through you. With the release of any negative feelings associated with heartbreak, you will begin to feel a renewed sense of self within growing stronger and stronger. Indifference brings to bear the temperance of said feelings.

Now, when I'm out in nature, observing the grandiose beauty of it all, I can literally feel everything around me that was created without any of my help, input, or thought of how I "felt" about its' creation. It is here that I can see and affirm the fact that the Universe needs NO help, my dear. Just as it brings you to it, it will just as effortlessly bring you through it.

All of your pain shall pass! That's the beauty in the transforming power of pain. How you come out of that fire is the only thing we should intently focus on.

Say it with your chest, Hun, bitter who? Not Us!

Wait.... He said what? 6

Now imagine, Sis, after all the hard work you've managed to put into cultivating a better you by growing through your painful moments and taking the time to learn from those experiences, only to have all of that hard work threatened by a less evolved human being. Doesn't sound too foreign does it? Nope! Because this type of shit happens every day. We've all encountered someone who's never put in an ounce of work towards creating a better version of themselves.

I'm talking about the potential threat from those who have made a lifelong career of playing the blame game. The ones who have moved throughout their lives, pointing the finger at everybody else while deflecting blame for their own self-imposed choices, which ultimately resulted in disaster after disaster.

Can you see someone like this bringing their representative to the table, allowing you to see what only they want you to see until they've finally gained your trust and a coveted position in your life? If the answer is yes, then we're on the same page. This behavior, my dear, is typical of a common gaslighter. A gaslighter will threaten severe damage to all of the PEACE you've worked so diligently to cultivate for yourself. I've encountered quite a few during my lifetime. It is only now, at this age and stage of life's juncture, that I know how to spot them before they can lift a hand to reach for a seat at my table.

If you're not familiar with the term "gaslighting" we're about to get real familiar with it Sis. As we delve into this chapter and start to discuss this common personality trait in depth, we will also explore the tactics and methodology associated with gaslighting so you too will know how to spot it when you see it. I will say this, Sis: if you have taken in anything I've discussed thus far, I implore you from the bottom of my soul to keep your head on swivel and your heart on notice as we dig into the character traits outlined in this chapter.

The ability to obtain a thorough understanding of them will likely save you a great amount of heartache and pain in the future. I can confidently guarantee you that! However, before we go in, let's take a step back to properly acknowledge your own intuitive God-like nature. Let's give it up for your innate goddess within and all of the tools we often suppress to make others feel comfortable.

For one, there is that inner compass (voice within) that guides you. You've heard it before, Sis, it's there for a reason. It's the closest thing to GOD in the flesh; that inner voice is there when you cannot hear the red flag whispers on the outside. Learn to pay attention to your internal compass: it's easy to dismiss. As a matter of fact, gaslighters have mastered the art of leading you to ignore not only your intuition but your other God-given senses as well.

IF you feel it in your core, it's there for a reason. Before you dismiss it, please know that a spiritual tap on the shoulder has the capacity to turn into the force of a 12-gauge shotgun blow to the chest. Let's work on paying attention to it earlier versus later.

[1]Gaslighting - a tactic in which a person or entity, in order to gain more power, makes a victim question their reality. It works much better than you may think. Anyone is susceptible to gaslighting, and it is a common technique of abusers, dictators, narcissists, and cult leaders. It is done slowly, so the victim doesn't realize how much they've been brainwashed.

Below are some of the most common techniques used by gaslighters:

1. They tell blatant lies intentionally to set a precedent. The lies make you unsure of any and everything they've said. This, in turn, keeps you unsteady and off kilter in your perceptions, which is their main goal.
2. They deny they have ever said something to you, even if you can prove it to the contrary. This tactic is designed to make you start questioning your reality. The more they do this, the more you question your reality, foregoing what you know and accepting their reality.
3. They use the things you hold dear as ammunition against you. See, gaslighting is done gradually over time and is designed to slowly chip away at you. This may even take shape in the attack of your kids, parents, and close friends. They negatively dissect the people around you in an effort to project their negative ideas onto you.

---

[1] https://www.psychologytoday.com/us/blog/here-there-and-everywhere/201701/11-warning-signs-gaslighting

4. They tell half-truths to align others against you. This tactic is to bring your sanity into question so when you finally reveal that this person is abusive or out of control, those claims are usually dismissed. It's one of their BEST techniques.
5. They project. They are constantly accusing you of being the source of discord. You then spend so much time trying to defend yourself that you are distracted from their own toxic behavior.

Have you seen any of this, Sis? Does it look familiar?

I know it does because I've experienced it myself – up close and personal – primarily in my romantic relationships. For the longest time, I never knew what the proper term for this madness was or how to even approach it. In those moments, you know what you know but the gaslighter throws so much confusion into the mix, using semantics and the art of exclusion so that by the end of the day, you are questioning yourself, "Damn, am I tripping?" Yes, my dear, I too have been there and done that. This right here is why so many people stay in abusive, volatile relationships. Many have no idea that this form of manipulation is being used on them. We gotta stay AWAKE, Sis. Awareness is critical because if you can't recognize it when you're in it, it has the potential to have lasting detrimental effects on your wellbeing, oftentimes lasting long after the relationship is over.

The last time I found myself knee-deep in this kind of situation, tried and true to the intended outcome, things went so horribly wrong between that person and me. It resulted in me being completely afraid to tell the truth, MY truth about MY experience with this person out of fear that no one would believe some of the traumatizing things that had actually transpired within our relationship.

Honestly, I still question it myself. There are many things I won't speak of in detail here; I still cannot believe that I put myself in a position, repeatedly, for such unspeakable things to occur. I just can't wrap my psyche around my unwillingness to leave in those moments. Although I know in reality that it happened, the whole situation left me very confused, emotionally scarred, and full of self-doubt. Despite the fact that I witnessed it firsthand, the severity of pain I endured was something I could never have fathomed allowing in my life. It was during those reflective moments when I realized that I'd been LIT by my gaslighter. By the time I realized what had occurred, I was still stuck, pondering a line that became synonymous in our relationship. "Wait, he said what?" "Did he REALLY just say that?"

I'm serious when I say I'd spend hours upon hours trying to "decode" the intricacies of the gaslighting that took place. During this time, my self-confidence was in the toilet! I no longer trusted myself and what I knew to be true. I didn't trust my heart or the feelings that urged me early on to let go of being so in love with this person. Most importantly, I no longer trusted my intuition. I've always been intuitively inclined, and those gut instincts had never ever led me in the wrong direction, ever in my life. Yet, I'd begun to doubt my own inner GOD, only to have it revealed to me after months of gaslighting... my spirit was right all along. Just as it always is, Sis.

Trust me, you will encounter plenty of people throughout your life who will attempt to bring their baggage, emotional instability, and mental chaos into your life. These people will literally attempt to drop all their bullshit off at your doorstep and expect you to unpack all their mess in the name of "Love."

If I've learned nothing over the years, I have definitively learned that you cannot simply "love" someone out of their bag-carrying ways. They are more likely to drag you down before you can pull them up! With all their weighted bullshit, Sis, your days of being a professional bag handler will surely drag you down and can inadvertently destroy everything you've managed to build for yourself. I'm talking about those sinking situations that have the ability to level your finances, rob you of career advancements, push out stable friendships, and take a very unhealthy toll on your physical state.

This is exactly why I am a staunch advocate for loving, what I like to call "anchors," from a distance. There is nothing wrong with creating barriers with someone from a far more manageable and protective distance. And if they cannot understand your choice of self- preservation in the face of their mess, it is time to level their expectations. This is where you have the right to set your own boundaries and guard your shit like Fort Knox. When it comes to maintaining your peace and sanity, carrying someone else's baggage should be a non-negotiable. You have to guard your shit with the ferocity of a pit bull, Sis! You are your own gatekeeper. The job of cultivating and maintaining peace in your life belongs to you and only you. I'd never recommend turning over that much power to another human being.

If someone is doing to you what I've just discussed in this chapter, it is time for you to GO, hun. Get the hell out and do not look back. You don't need to proclaim your emancipation either... a plan is all about execution and strategy. The less they know or anticipate, the better off you'll be when it comes to making a clean break. To be honest, it is not even worth the effort to confront a gaslighter about their behavior. Trust me, many gaslighters are M-A-S-T-E-R-S of manipulation.

I simply ask that you trust yourself and your God-given strength to move accordingly. If that means exiting the situation all together, please do. There will probably be people around you who question you, especially if they are not privy to the mental abuse of the gaslighter in your life. However, I ask that you allow those opinions to fall on deaf ears. No one will protect you like you. The bottom line: If it does not feel right, it ain't right. Period. Allow your inner GOD talk to be your guiding force. To keep it real, I say FUCK the opinions of others when it comes to protecting your emotional, physical, and mental health. If you do find yourself in a scenario like this, it could easily become a matter of life and death. Please stay diligent and, most importantly, please stay away! Take it from me. You cannot save them, leave that work to Jesus.

P.S. you ain't Jesus, Sis. ~ signed with love.

Options   7

One of the most beautiful words in the English language is the word, OPTIONS. I talk to my two young boys often about the choices they will be faced with in this lifetime and their ability to choose wisely in reviewing and exercising their options. Just the sound of "options" fills my soul with a strong feeling of immense gratitude, knowing that I have the ability to CHOOSE most things I allow in my life. Think about it. There are so many things in life we have little to no control over, whatsoever. Then there are the things we have all the power and dominion over. That choice is yours! You can get with this, or you can get with that. Beautiful concept, isn't it? You have the POWER to decide what you will tolerate, what you're capable of tolerating, and, most importantly, what's simply a hard " NO" for you personally. No matter the decision queen, the choice is all up to you.

You can choose to cultivate peace, serenity, and all things Zen in your life if you want. To play it fair, you can even have a little joy, mixed with a tidbit of chaos (don't knock it; some people need just a taste) nicely woven in between moments of soul-comforting trap music, pumpkin spice lattes, and good lovin' from an amicable friends with benefits situation - if you see fit!

Say it with me again, options! See, once you fully grasp the concept that you do not have to tolerate anyone's messiness, negativity, misplaced issues, worries, fears, or other bullshit that makes your spirit tingle with disgust, it is in this space that you find true liberation. You don't owe anyone who's incapable of reciprocating your efforts or contributing to your growth a designated spot in your life. No, ma'am, I am here to reaffirm that you do not owe them shit.

To take it a step further, you don't even owe anyone an explanation of your boundaries. Now, if you decide you want to find an eloquent way of explaining your choice to draw imaginary lines in the sand, as a measure of being considerate to the other's party's feelings, then I say fine. Do what works best for you. However, if further contact with this person (place or thing) is far more detrimental to your peace than you're willing to allow, no explanation is necessary. Just cut it, ASAP. No long, drawn-out proclamation is needed when you've reached this point. Now, this doesn't mean embark on a rampant spree, attempting to remove everything you deem to be painful impediments all at once. I can easily see the situation becoming highly overwhelming and super emotional very fast. The choice to move on or rise above harmful situations shouldn't be a mental or emotional death sentence. While cutting out the potentially harmful things in your life, remember that pain may be a necessary evil at that moment.

Think about it! Most of us only change in uncomfortable situations. Those painful spaces in our lives are usually where we have the most profound periods of growth. The directive here, Sis, is reinforcing the fact that YOU can choose what experiences you allow. You are not obligated or indebted to anyone so much that you completely forego your own best interests in lieu of someone else's. I cannot emphasize enough how important self-preservation is when it comes to maintaining a sound mental space.

I'm sure there are many of us who have felt trapped in situations, maybe even romantic relationships, where we didn't feel like leaving was a viable choice to make at the time. Some will choose to stay and cheat on their partner instead. Others may choose to stay and purposely attempt to make someone's life miserable because they're incapable of removing themselves from that perpetual wheel of hurt. Some will even stay because of their own self-induced fear of the unknown. I'm here to tell you none of this is absolute law, Sis. You don't owe anyone a miserable existence, and you are not required to subject yourself to it. The power of free will says that you can consciously make a decision based on the options presented to you, while weighing them on your own personal scale of importance, as to which choices produce the most positive outcome. You are not here to be a mental slave or prisoner to anyone's expectations.

Society has imprinted on our mental canvas that suffering is synonymous with living. The lies have told us that if we wait long enough, coupled with the anticipation that someone else will choose for us, in the end everything will be okay. I'm here to tell you that it's all a trick, Sis. You do not have to willingly participate in someone else's version of the reindeer games. I'd like to think you'd want so much better for yourself. I know I did, which is what prompted a shift in my thinking. We all have to start somewhere, but now that you know the choice is yours, make a promise to yourself to always CHOOSE WISELY!

EXERCISE 2.0

List 3 things you feel obligated to do for someone other than yourself within the next couple of weeks.

1. _____

2. _____

3. _____

List 3 things you WANT to do within the next couple of weeks.

1. _____

2. _____

3. _____

Now compare the two list and ask yourself these fundamental questions:

Are the things you feel obligated to do absolutely necessary?
_____
_____

What will happen if you don't do one or all the obligatory things you've listed?
_____
_____

Will the energy you exert in performing these tasks fulfill you in anyway?
_____
_____

Does your obligated task relate to your purpose and/or your passion in life?
_____
_____

If you answer no to any of the questions above, then why are you making these things a priority in your life? Try to swap at least one of your obligatory duties per week with something you want and CHOOSE to do! There must be a healthy balance in place. Putting the needs and wants of others above your own isn't a healthy practice for anyone. Remember that the right to choose is yours! The world will not crumble if you choose yourself for once. As women we tend to sacrifice our own needs, forsaking our goals, passions and dreams in lieu of supporting those around us. In life, there needs to be a continuous flow of energy. If you are pouring into everyone else without refilling your own cup you will find yourself deprived mentally, physically and just outright emotionally depleted.

POUR UP... before you breakdown. Your cup is your source so how can you allow yourself to go thirsty? Give this some real thought, Queen, because no one will show up for you better than you. ♥

That's all MAGIC   8

It is the magnificent glory of a woman in all her splendor, beautifully and wonderfully made. She is a specially-crafted gem known as one of God's most precious creations. She is amazing in her ways, perfectly flawed and all. How blessed she is to be pure magic in the flesh, truly a sight to behold!

You've been deposited onto this earth with a purpose and all the necessary means needed to bring forth that divine purpose. Know, first and foremost, that you are special. You are created in the likeness of GOD. Each one of us was crafted in our own special way. We possess the innate ability to charter our own courses through life, giving form to our individual creativity as a vessel to bring to fruition every dream, every goal, and every purpose-filled desire one's heart could ever imagine.

You my dear are POWERFUL - far beyond words! Every curvature. Every mole. Every freckle and even that strand of hair that always seems to fall out of formation. You, my dear, are MARVELOUS. I'm talking molasses dipped, thick and dripping in tassels of gold, glazed in silkiness, sheer perfection personified!

You, my Queen, are a BAD ONE! I truly mean this, Sis. I'm not here to sell falsities. My father use to say, "No one will ever buy into your idea of you if you don't buy in first." There is absolutely nothing wrong with knowing you are the shit and believing it with every fiber of your being. Usually, efforts to contradict this line of thinking perpetuate the idea that you are supposed to dim your light to allow others to shine.

There is nothing wrong with humility; it's a beautiful characteristic to embody. However, I've personally witnessed backlash from what others perceive as being less than "humble", especially if your unfuckwithableness is operating at a higher frequency. Some folks just can't handle that. It makes them feel uncomfortable, so the expectation is for you to dim your light to ease their level of comfort. With all due respect, Sis, I say fuck all that. Plain and simple.

How does your level of confidence affect you? This is the question I'd pose to anyone who insists that, as women, we must learn to "be a bit more humble". If your aura vibrates with respect and courtesy to others (I'd say to always make it your goal to be kind when and where you can, as kindness to self and others is so important) and if you're leading with love and trying daily to build a bridge of understanding, I say do it, Sis, and do it WELL. When I think back to all the times I didn't feel worthy of the ground I stood on, I'm filled with a spirit of immense gratitude in my soul.

I've come to realize that despite being at my lowest and feeling unworthy of living, I survived those things designed to tear me down. Not only did I survive, as a testament to my survival, I continually strive to whip my muthafuckin' hair every single chance I get. My journey of learning to embrace my own MAGIC would never allow me to use it in a way to willfully and purposely diminish someone else's light.

This ain't about them, Sis! This is about you and knowing that no matter what life throws at you, no matter who comes forth to tear you down - in character or in the flesh - you are a force to be reckoned with; and anyone who knows you, knows that energy cannot be destroyed.

As a child, I hated the shape of my nose. I absolutely loathed my side profile. I hated my hair. It was too curly and thick, and completely unmanageable. The more I focused on the things I hated, the more pronounced they became. Soon, these perceived atrocities began to cost me a lot of excess time daily, trying either to hide, mask, or cover them up. Inadvertently, I actually started to draw attention to them even more. Like the time I pulled my curly tresses back tight and packed on about 10 oz's of Ampro hair gel, along with ten scrunchy ties, to hide my waves. I walked around that whole day with my eyes slanted and snatched all the way to heaven. It was all good until a childhood friend asked me in front of everybody why was I walking around looking like my name was Ling Lee.

I remember thinking to myself that day, "Damn, you did all of that excessiveness to try to change your appearance; and low and behold, someone still found a problem with it." That's life, Sis, in a nutshell. Someone will ALWAYS have a problem with something. You cannot appease everyone, and neither should you try. If you wake up in the AM and feel like FLEXIN', do it. You can never overdose on self-love. It's the gift that keeps on giving. In fact, having an ample amount of self-love opens the gateway to exerting genuine love for each other. Don't believe me? Try it.

Lastly, no one who walks this earth who will be a more magical version of you than you. So, I invite you to live as loud and pronounced in your essence as possible. It is important that you not only formulate strong positive ideas of yourself but also reinforce these ideas with positive affirmations. This way, no one else can ever tell you who or what you are NOT. And believe me, there will be those in this life who will try to defeat you with their narrow-minded ideas of what you can and cannot achieve in this lifetime, what you should and should not look like, etc.

We have come to know these types as "haters"; however, I challenge that label. I say, let's not assign them a title with such negative connotations. After all, what then would make us any different? Learn to fight the negative with the positive. I've learned that you will attract way more bees with sugar than salt!

We will simply say, "They must NOT KNOW WHO YOU ARE?" They are the ones who come forth as doubters and non-believers - those who challenge your vision of yourself and act as if you are not wonderfully comprised of all things magic. Baby, I am here to let you know that you have everything necessary to draw your own self portrait! Let them marvel in the finished product and trust me when I say their eyes will most certainly be watching.

Gone girl, give em' a show!

For as magical as you are love, please keep in mind:

"Beauty isn't about having a pretty face. It is about having a pretty mind, a pretty heart and most importantly a beautiful soul."

- Dr. Kesirju Ramprasad

EXERCISE 3.0

Take a Moment! List 5 things that you would consider absolutely magical about yourself outside of any physical attribute. Dig deep, Sis. I want to see the inner you on the outside.

1. _____
_____
2. _____
_____
3. _____
_____
4. _____
_____
5. _____
_____

Now, let's go even deeper! List 5 things about you that you'd like to add to your magical essence. These could be inner or outer attributes you aspire to improve.

1. _____
_____
2. _____
_____

3. _____
   _____

4. _____
   _____

5. _____
   _____

Remember to be kind to yourself, Sis! We all have areas to improve, so take into consideration where you've come from and look ahead to where you desire to be. Now formulate an effective plan to close that gap. Revisit your plan daily and make revisions as often as you deem necessary.

It's okay to rewrite and/or redirect your path to greatness. No one person (or, specifically here, one woman) is perfect, but we are perfectly designed in our essence to become our individual reflection of perfection.

Beauty in the Struggle

9

I remember when I bought my first home in 2016. When I pulled into the driveway awaiting my realtor's arrival, I couldn't help but smile at the captivating beauty of the rose bush that was perched beautifully on the lawn right near the front entrance. The colors were so bold and vibrant. I remember thinking to myself, "Whoever planted this bush certainly planted it with love" because the rose bush had blossomed into an amazing piece of eye-catching beauty. It was definitely a great selling point for the modestly-sized home before me. After viewing the home with my realtor, as I pulled out of the driveway, I glanced once more at that rose bush. In that very moment, I knew this was the home I'd live in one day. I'll admit that after the purchase, as the years went by, I did not maintain that rose bush the least bit. The only seeds I have ever been interested in planting and watering are those in the soul and spirit.

Your girl does NOT have a green thumb and that's for damn sure. It's plainly evident in the now-withering rose bush that sits in my front yard, a handful of petals clinging on for dear life. Specifically, one winter we had a pretty heavy snowfall for Georgia, not nearly as bad as those I'd experienced growing up in the Midwest, but it proved to be completely immobilizing for the Metro Atlanta area. I sat near my front window that day and watched as my rose bush got semi-pummeled by snow. In the days that followed, it appeared that the bush was a goner. It had cracked, splitting right near the base and was now leaning on a deep slope. I was convinced that was all she wrote for that poor little bush. I'd even begun looking to hire a landscaper to replant another one in its place. However, as the days went by, the leaning rose bush began to perk back up a bit, showing me it still had a little life left in it after all. In the weeks that followed, I noticed one or two more buds forming on the struggling bush. As those tiny buds began to bloom, I thought to myself, "Wow, even as the bush is clearly struggling, I can still see small shining remnants of its beauty."

My observation of the rose bush is a great way to approach how we assess our own individual struggles in life. Even as our heaviest burdens weigh us down with life happenings that feel almost impossible to recover from, if we can hone in on our innate ability to survive and evolve, despite those weights, we can begin to see our spiritual rose buds bloom.

We must allow our vibrancy to shine through our toughest times, exposing our beauty even in the face of adversity. Gaining insight and understanding from a natural occurrence in nature reinforced a feeling I'd long felt in my spirit: at the very brink of destruction, when it comes to pure survival, is where we find our true strength.

The ugliest times in our lives tend to take our focus away from the glory that occurs amid the struggle. It's long been said that the calmest place is in the very middle of the storm. There is beauty right there in the pit of chaos if we learn to calm ourselves and actively find the peace around us.

Although it may feel like we're surrounded by complete chaos, when you learn to surrender, you can acknowledge with full awareness that those moments of chaos, pain, suffering and stress are just that – passing moments in time. These moments will surely pass just as the sun gives way to night, only to rise again for the next dawn. Just as night passes, so shall any chaos we experience in any moment. To prove what I'm saying here in simplicity, close your eyes. Imagine the most painful thing you have ever encountered. Visualize the pain you felt, the confusion, the disappointment, the depression, the physical weariness, and anxiety you endured in that space in time.

Now, open your eyes and yourself to full awareness of where you are right now. Feel, the now-ness and newness of the chair you're sitting in, feel the cushion of the foot stool you may have your feet propped up in as you're reading. Inhale and exhale and feel the air around you. Do you feel that? Do you know what it is? I'll tell you exactly what it is: it is NOT that painful moment that you endured before. This is where you are now, and you are not there anymore. That's the Beauty!

Despite the misconceptions we all have at some point regarding the struggling and/or suffering we go through in life, I am here to tell you, Sis, no matter what the issue is, you must know that first and foremost everyone goes through struggles in life. Again, you are not alone. Personalizing our struggles keeps us tied to that perpetual wheel of victimization. We must make a conscious effort to change our perceptions regarding our struggles. Dark times do not last longer than we allow. To keep it all real for you, IF you allow yourself to wallow in the pain, and if you allow those negative feelings to linger and fester, it has the potential to weigh you down heavily; and from a mental standpoint ,that can land you in a very bad place.

There are people in this world everyday who never recover from that place. I've personally had family member commit suicide when their personal struggles became too much to bear. So, while you have the ability to recognize the undertow in your pain, your entire objective should be to stay above the water, even during your bleakest hours, so it doesn't drag you off-square and out of this life.

"How can I stay positive and aware when I'm hurting so bad inside?" I've asked this question a gazillion times over. Why? Because I've been to the bottomless pit of pain, the deepest depths of struggle and faced the unrelenting grip of strife for what seemed like a large part of my life. I've walked it, Sis, and I'm still here. So, I can talk it! I can honestly admit it's hard as fuck to cultivate a positive thought when you're dealing with internal turmoil.

Note: I said it was hard, not impossible. A key thing for me has always been to find a nurturing place to center myself. Sometimes, I'd sneak into my sons' bedroom while they were sleeping. I'd sit among their quiet loving space, soaking up every ounce of it because I knew they love me unconditionally. No matter what issues I was dealing with inside, I knew my children loved and adored me. So, I'd take those moments, often sitting in complete darkness and listen to them breathe as they slept, sometimes even placing my hand over their hearts to simply feel their beating. In those moments I'd repeat this mantra to myself in soft whisper...

"I am because I can. Nothing can come forth to stop me but me. Nothing can break me unless I allow. Yes, my current state is hurt but I know my end state is Peace. My end state is Freedom, from this very moment."

Rinse and repeat, literally! Many times, the tears streaming from my face would begin to wash away the pain as I allowed myself to simply release it.

I'd repeat this mantra as many times as needed until I not only felt its release, but until I BELIEVED deep down in the core of my being my pain had been removed. Wholly and solely. Surrounded by the invisible yet undeniable love from my children, I used their strength to add a little fuel to my own. And you can do this wherever you consider your "safe" place. I'd say to ensure it's a place that allows you the freedom to be your most vulnerable self. My cousin confessed that she'd do something similar at her mother's gravesite. I've found myself repeating this mantra at my workplace, tucked away in a bathroom stall. Albeit it's not the most ideal location, but I when I needed an immediate relief from the workplace chaos, the bathroom is where I'd retreat.

I kid you not, after summoning forth my moment of awareness, "stepping into the now," I instantly began to see the colors around me just a bit brighter. I'd find myself focusing on a stitch of fabric in the carpet or a painting seen through my office door, and for some reason things seemed more vibrant. I noticed the most finite detail, and in those small intricacies I'd find beauty. Have you ever really – intently – just sat in silence listening to a clock as it ticks? When you're in a heightened state of awareness, even the ticking hands of a clock can sound like a joyous melodic note. Listen, focus, and find the beauty! It's there, I swear.

EXERCISE 4.0

As you go throughout your day:, take note of 5 things around you that you may not have noticed before. In your moment of acknowledgement, can you see something intriguing, powerful, or intrinsically beautiful about it?

1. _____

2. _____

3. _____

4. _____

5. _____

Paid in Full — 10

This life owes you nothing, Sis. I know you may be thinking that's a pretty bold statement, right? And I, in no way, intend to be overly brash or insensitive, but it is the God-honest truth, Queen. A lot of us get caught up in the idea that we were dealt "a bad hand" in life, especially when we're so often faced with many different challenges on our journey. It's easier to look over the fence at someone else's life and make a judgment that their path in life was not as tumultuous and/or trying as ours. Under this mindset, it could feel like you've been unfairly targeted. It's easy to assume that some higher power has taken up a personal vendetta against you. Just as I said before and I'll say many times to come, NONE of what happens to you, directly or indirectly, is ever really personal.

Now, this is not to say that we don't play a role in bringing about unpleasant outcomes. Experiencing a hardship (or two) that results from our own actions is simply cause and effect, and there is an effect (be it good or bad) for every cause. See, everything we do directly influences our lives, even though we may know in our heart of hearts that the possible outcomes will have a negative impact, is a clear example of that cause-and-effect flow I'm speaking about. At the end of the day, life is life. Your road is your road. Yes, it may be tough, but who ever said that it would be easy? That's a psychological concept perpetuated by Disney fairytales and Tyler Perry movies. No one person walking this earth is immune to trials and tribulations. Ever heard the saying, "life is cold, but it's fair"? Maybe not fair by your standards, if you only reason from your own biased perspective. But I promise you that everything you encounter is specifically designed to grow you in a way that only a certain level of discomfort and pain can. And growth, Sis, is what we're all put here to do! Life is a course of ever-evolving growth mentally, physically, spiritually, and emotionally. This is exactly what I see when I look back on every perceived "bad hand" I've been dealt in my life.

There was a time during my teenager years when I was involved in a very abusive relationship. I was 15 when I became involved with my abuser. Although we weren't intimate until I was 16, he was 19 and considered a young adult. Oh, my God, he was so damn charming! He was immensely hilarious and quite handsome. These were the things that attracted me to him. And now I know my insecurities of being a skinny, flat-chested introvert were some of the reasons why I was elated he showed an interest in me.

He eventually become my first boyfriend. Now, many people can recount their first love or first romance with fond memories that spark beautiful feelings of nostalgia. The "firsts" typically conjure up memories that we keep as pivotal points of self-discovery in our lives. As for me and my first love experience? Well, my situation wasn't quite that way. While I learned some of my best lessons during this situation early in life, whenever I am around my girlfriends, reminiscing about our past loves, I can't help but feel cheated to a certain degree. My first love story didn't start out with that idealistic, romantic nostalgia. My first boyfriend physically and mentally abused me so badly that I still grappled with the effects of that traumatic period for well over 20 years.

I endured horrific beatings at the hands of this man for approximately 18 months before something got a hold of me long enough to whisper to my spirit, "Baby girl, this isn't love." I can recall the happenings surrounding that revealing moment. A little over a year into the relationship, he'd kicked, slapped, choked, and punched me savagely, resulting in not one but two black eyes. He reached new heights of disrespect when he intentionally spat on me during a heated exchange. I knew that there was only so much I could endure. Towards the end of the relationship, I finally gathered enough courage to face him and tell him I wanted out of the relationship. I was around 17 by that time. I came to the realization that I was far too young to be in such an adult-like situation. I hid the abuse from those closest to me. I was estranged from my crack cocaine-addicted mother for most of my teenage years. Although my father and I are much closer now, we weren't quite seeing eye to eye or really speaking during this abusive time.

However, I'd finally decided I had enough of the black eyes and bruises, and I no longer wanted to live in fear of my life with a man who clearly, in hindsight, had serious psychological issues. So, I mustered up every ounce of strength I could find inside my young, petite frame and found myself weeping a river of tears as I stood face-to-face with my first love, attempting to reasonably explain why I was leaving him.

I even tried to appeal to his so-called love for me by adding how I didn't deserve to be treated this way when all I ever tried to do was be a caring girlfriend. I found myself further expressing how bad it hurt me when he'd hit me and verbally degraded me. I mean I poured my little naïve heart out to this man, who literally sat in front of me in complete silence, calmly, as he continued to puff on a cigarette. Looking back on it, I should have gotten my ass up out of there at that very moment. Instead, I stood there awaiting a courteous response from a man who'd never shown any courtesy or kindness to me in any way.

That kind of naiveté right there, as a young woman, can lead you to ruin and, as an older woman, indicates that you obviously haven't learned much of anything over the course of your life. If you really believe that your abuser isn't aware of the pain and/or damage their abuse causes, there is something to be said about your own feelings of self-worth. Believing that you can fix or save your abuser will only destroy you. That mindset is the reason why I stood as still as a statue that day as I attempted to explain my exit plan to someone who'd always felt entitled to possess me at any cost.

He continued his calm demeanor, finishing his cigarette, still not uttering a single word. After a few awkward minutes passed, he finally got up, walked three steps over to me and stood so close that I could feel his breath on my eyelids. True to his nature, just as he'd done many times before, without uttering a word, he reached his hand up and grabbed me by my neck with what I could only describe as every single ounce of strength he had inside of him. As a matter of fact, had I not been privy to his level of rage from our prior abusive encounters, I swear I would have passed out at that very moment. It felt like a python had wrapped itself around my neck and was hell-bent on inducing my demise. I clawed at his hands in an attempt to loosen the fingers gripped around my neck. I'd learned before not to exert too much energy fighting him off, as I would surely need every ounce of air to withstand his constriction of my airways.

In those brief moments, I felt my life flash before my eyes and, simultaneously, I had an out-of-body experience. I could literally see myself on the sidelines, watching this man choke the life out of me. It was then that I knew this could never be a part of my reality again. How did I end up here? *Fighting for my life, feeling worthless and deserving of the treatment this person handed me. How did I ever manage to sign myself up for such treatment?* These were very real questions I knew were necessary to confront. I knew this had become a crucial turning point in my transition into womanhood because if I continued to make excuses using my simple-minded understanding of love as a kickstand for my inability to love myself more, I knew this would not be the last time I'd endure painful situations of this magnitude.

Needless to say, I made it out of that situation although not without some emotional scars that I still carry. I know that trusting myself forced me to define what it is "I" desired for my life. I had to learn where to start breaking the previous ideologies of what I deserved. You see, that's the silent narrative, once again, amongst women (primarily women of color) that obligates us to suffer and sacrifice for some greater reward down the line. This plays out in almost all our relationships across a wide spectrum of our lives. How many people have you witnessed who are fully committed to remaining in loveless marriages full of infidelity, lies, disrespect, and abuse all in the name of "Love"?

Sis, tell me how many do you personally know? And don't worry; I'll wait! I want you to take a moment and take inventory of these kind of harmful relationships you've encountered thus far. I am positive that you've witnessed this scenario among some of your friends, family members, and even colleagues, if not falling prey to it yourself. The question I pose here is, "Who says that suffering in the name of love has to be YOUR narrative?"

Sis, the thing is life doesn't owe you anything! Consider your struggles as paid debts to your old framework of thinking. As long as you have breath in your body, you can consistently revise and rewrite your path. This is the beauty born within your soul. Once you understand, with pen in hand and your mental psyche as the canvas, you, my dear, are practically unstoppable. How can you even consider remaining a slave to your past experiences and traumas when the ability to erase and revise is a gift bestowed upon you from God.

The beauty is that it's right there within you. Just as I've made the commitment to work on revising my path daily, consider your past traumas as Paid in Full. You don't owe anyone payment by offering yourself as a sacrifice amid their bullshit. Since life owes you nothing in return, please stop accepting their pain in hopes of a future reward.

EXERCISE 5.0

Repeat the mantra below when and wherever you can. Feel it in the depths of your spirit and speak it with conviction.

"I am not my past and I am not your pain.
Today I make the commitment to cultivate myself on fertile ground.
I will NOT uproot my harvest to feed your destruction.
I AM healthy, hearty, and full in mind, body, and spirit.
Chaos and confusion can no longer sit in my presence at this table.
I release you, and I wish you well on your way."

Marathon Runner II

" Life is not a sprint, it's a Marathon." I think we've all heard this saying before, yet how many of us truly understood it?

I've only been on this earth for three decades and some change, but I've come to realize the overwhelming importance of mapping a clear, concise path and properly pacing yourself. Many of us start out on this race of life, running fast and strong. Right out of the gate, we hit the ground at 100 miles an hour straight gunnin' it! We set out with aspirations to tackle this vast world and all it has to offer in one fell swoop - fueled by pure adrenaline, combined with the newfound reality of our freedom, which, in our inexperienced eyes, represents unlimited potential for us. Armed with the bright-eyed beliefs that tell us the sky is the limit and we can do anything we set our minds to, we muscle up every ounce of energy and go at life full force.

It's like being fresh out of high school. Some of us go off to college while some, like me, make our run for a spot in the workplace. We tend to spend lavishly, seeking out all things pleasurable, desirable, and exciting to our untrained minds. Some of us settle down early, buying homes and starting families, while riding that corporate ladder bullet straight to the top.

In moments like this, everything seems so fast-paced. It's almost as if we're being checked by some imaginary clock as we run laps on life's obstacle course. However, in our haste to conquer, we make waste. We make bad decisions in love, often choosing partners based on what we think we want versus what we actually need. We make bad financial decisions, racking up mounds of debt so early on that we spend decades trying to recover and find a new level of financial security. Some of us make bad life decisions in general as we run through unhealthy habit after unhealthy habit. We forego our passions and purpose in pursuit of the cushy confines we believe the corporate world will offer us.

For instance, and I'll use myself as an example, my passion has always been writing. For as far back as I can remember, growing up in a household that was the epitome of dysfunction, I used my knack for writing to paint vivid pictures in my head, creating tales of grandeur that I'd use as a form of escapism from the chaos in which I lived. Of course, the stories I wrote usually reflected the exact opposite views of my reality. I'd write from the perspective of a little girl who had a present mother, and a child who had a good, hot meal every night. This child had a nice warm bed of her own to sleep in, not the rinky-dink metal cot I actually slept on in my grandmother's dining room. I made sure that my stories were a stark contrast to my actual surroundings.

Although I grew up in a house full of love, provided by my grandparents, it was also a house full of demons, courtesy of everyone else in our immediate and extended family construct. My grandparents were from the Deep South, and with them came those deep southern traditions, ideals, and what I call family "curses". We were raised under many unspoken covenants. One rule that I'd been strictly conditioned to abide by was the fact that family business was family business to be kept amongst family.

We were taught not to air our dirty laundry out in the streets. I'd often overhear these little secrets within the family by eavesdropping on my grandmother's conversations with her sisters. I was too young to really understand the magnitude of the discussions but old enough to know it wasn't for me to repeat outside of our house. I often tell people that my family had more secrets than the Brotherhood of Freemasons. Some of those very secrets crept into my bed at night, robbing me of my innocence at a young age. Unwilling to continue how I'd been taught, I did eventually tell my mother what happened to me on two separate occasions by two different adult male relatives.

Of course, the things I told her never left the house. Although the abuse stopped, the trauma was never addressed, just like many of the secrets that lay hidden behind the walls of 736 W. 61st Place. Those traumatic experiences growing up are what pushed me deeper into writing the stories that allowed me to escape the barriers of my physical confines.

I learned that I could go almost anywhere in my mind. As I honed my writing skills, my stories became more and more elaborate, painting a fairytale existence that I looked forward to in adulthood. If I had a dime for every time I told myself, "I can't wait to grow up," I can assure you I'd likely be financially set for life.

I dreamed of life as an adult, knowing that once I was in full control and free to pursue whatever dream I could conjure up, my life would be so much better. I turned 16 and was off like a runner at the start of a race. I left home early, experiencing adulthood much sooner than I was actually prepared for. Nonetheless, I relentlessly pursued that fairytale existence I'd dreamed of as a child. Bobbing and weaving in and out of traumatic experience after traumatic experience, I still managed to rack up some nice personal accomplishments along the way. I had my first apartment at 18, bought my first brand new car at 19, and was working a full-time job making more money than my friends who'd actually gone off to college.

You couldn't tell me nothing! I was moving at such a fast pace that I began to believe I would never run out of gas. Well, just as the natural laws predict, eventually it all came crashing down. Somewhere along the line, I forgot to stop and refill. I didn't know how to look at what was going on around me and truly live in those moments. All I could see was the imaginary finish line at the end of my race, except the closer I got to the line, the farther back the line moved.

I found myself chasing a ghost, so to speak. That finish line did not exist the way I had envisioned. There was no grand prize of peace, joy, happiness, or contentment waiting for me at the end of the line as I had fictitiously imagined it. As we all know, Sis, we don't get to say when we're finished with life and demand our parting gifts.

That's not how it works! None of us know when we're truly done with life, as we cannot predict the day we die. While we can set goals for ourselves and timelines according to when we'd like to accomplish these goals, trust me when I say that mark will continue to move as we go further along on our journeys. It is imperative for you to PACE YOURSELF!

Make it a goal to carve out time to celebrate those milestones you hit on your journey. Keep a constant line of revision working. As you probably already know, what you think you've mastered today, life has a way of showing that you, in fact, don't really know shit. We all think that if we continually acquire the things we diligently pursue, at some point, we'll finally be able to sit down and enjoy them.

I say, enjoy them NOW. Who's to say that you'll still be in the race tomorrow? Running so fast toward that finish line, I guarantee you'll run out of steam before you run out of dreams. They'll keep piling, and you'll keep running after them wildly until that moment (which nearly everyone I know has experienced) you look up and realize you've missed everything chasing all things.

Ask yourself, "What is important to me?" and ask this question often. We change our mindsets as we grow and evolve. Take inventory of all the things you've acquired. Take a moment to pat yourself on the back too, Sis! If you can look back over the course of your life and see distinct mental and emotional growth, you can mark off the goals you've already met and truly utilize those priceless lessons you've learned.

Give yourself a round of applause! No matter how big or how small; progress is progress! To live is to know how hard life can be at times. Why not take a quick rest stop to reflect on the key points you've made in your race? How will you know what direction to continue moving in if you haven't evaluated the direction of the route from which you've come?

Allow yourself a moment to stop and smell the roses. You cannot catch your breath if you are still sprinting in life's marathon, grabbing at every single thing you pass along the way. Although you've come a long way, and you may have started out swift and strong, you still have a long way to go, and the course is constantly changing. Slow it down a bit, Sis, remain present in the moment, and, most importantly, please remember to breathe.

I encourage you to keep moving forward, never give up during your life's marathon. Just learn to set a manageable pace that keeps you in it for the long haul.

EXERCISE 6.0

Name 3 things you've accomplished this year and how you celebrated those accomplishments.

1. _____
   _____
   _____

2. _____
   _____
   _____

3. _____
   _____
   _____

New levels, New (Social) Devils

12

> " May your rise back to the pinnacles of your own Greatness be just as talked about as your fall." Sis'latians 1:2

Can you specifically recall a moment in your life that you would characterize as your lowest of low points? No worries or judgment here, Sis. I have had several - far more than I care to recall in detail. The craziest thing is even in my lowest moments, I remember being more concerned about how weak or unstable I'd appear in the eyes of the outside world. It's funny how we claim not to care what others think, yet we live our lives in a glass box, trembling with fear and anticipating the next stone to be thrown our way. Downright bizarre, isn't it?

Everyone's happy and "living their best life" when we're on top, right? To the contrary, though, we cower in fear and sulk in shame and embarrassment when things fall apart, especially if our low points manage to make their way onto our social medi timelines. It's at that moment when our suffering becomes a highly publicized open market event. We manage to lose ourselves in the thoughts, opinions, judgments, and critiques of others. The same moments that many of us secretly wish we could shroud ourselves in complete cover and hide from the world have somehow managed to become open fodder for public opinion. This kind of open court melee has rarely produced or promoted any type of positive healing. While I've always considered myself a fairly private person, I can tell you that that was mostly out of fear. Fear built on the opinions and criticism of others. As strong as I professed to be, I'd always prided myself on being a strong feminine force who had ZERO problem defending and/or protecting myself.

But, baby, when I tell you nothing is more mentally taxing than falling apart while exposing your gaping wounds to society's prying eye. In 2018, I experienced one of the worst romantic breakups I'd been through since the breakdown of my marriage several years prior, which in hindsight paled in comparison to the excruciating mental anguish this more recent breakup caused me.

Although the breakdown and eventual dissolution of my marriage came with its share of pain and disappointments, I think experiencing another devastating separation was such a tremendous blow to my spirit because, once again, I thought I had it all figured out this time around. Before we physically split, I meticulously plotted the break from my ex-husband for an entire year before it actually came to fruition. As most women know, we typically start the emotional uncoupling as soon as we see actions that threaten to push us beyond our breaking point. To this point, the bond between my ex-husband and I had become irrevocably broken, leading to our split and the ultimate demise of our marriage. So, I did what I thought was the best form of coping, especially during those tumultuous times. I divested myself from that situation early on, which made the subsequent physical break a bit easier in the end.

However, the breakdown of my 2018 relationship completely brought me to my knees – literally and figuratively – because I was unable to break the emotional connection, even though I knew the relationship wouldn't serve either of us well in the long-term. During that break, my pain stemmed mostly from replaying how much time and energy I thought I'd consciously invested into being a better version of myself so that I could give the love I was also seeking. In my mind, I had this grand idea that if I actively worked on fixing me during my singlehood, I just knew that by the time a new opportunity to love presented itself, things would undoubtedly work out.

Why? Because I'd done what I thought was the necessary work, work that was mine alone to do to create in me (and my life) something new. My psyche just could not comprehend how, after all that, my relationship could still fail. The possibility wasn't even on my radar. A deeply-rooted spiritual connection came to an abrupt, although much needed, end in a very public manner. By "public", I'm specifically addressing the fallout with disconnecting friends, family and, of course, the eyes of the online world we'd allowed into so many aspects of our relationship via Facebook.

In subsequent months after the breakup, and while heavily indulged in my own self-healing phase, I'd found myself still privy to my ex's happenings via this world of people we'd so willingly invited into our lives when things were on the up and up. That's the thing here, Sis. You must remain cognizant that the same eyes watching you on your rise (whether it be career or relationship) will be the same set of eyes watching you when that pendulum swings back down to the lows of life's valleys. And you better believe, there is MUCH gossip and speculation on matters of how you live and handle your life. As I stated in earlier chapters, everyone will swear that they can live your life far better than you ever could!

Based on the popularity and growing pace of all things social media, I think we can all share similar stories of our own borderline obsessive behavioral patterns when it comes to the indulgence of social media platforms. However, we must also be aware of the detrimental harm we do to ourselves and others when fully immersed in a world that is not rooted in reality.

I'm sure you've witnessed the happenings of what appear to be a mental and/or emotional breakdown of someone on your friends list. It's highly likely we've all experienced the cries for help from someone linked to us through an IP address. Their pleas for either help, or in some cases attention, have bellowed into the abyss of social media during a moment of what can be described as obvious depression. Issues like this are laid out and played out for consumption and criticism of random strangers when they're best handled by a licensed professional. I'll go as far as to say that each of us has probably had our moments of internet pettiness, sadness, disappointments, disputes and other unfavorable dispositions that we'd take back if we could. And if you are not properly grounded in who you are, things left open for the world to criticize, often in the most inhumane way, can hurt you in more ways than you know.

I've often heard people say, "I don't care what the world thinks of me." This exact sentiment has pursed my lips a time or two. Now knowing what I know, I highly doubt that proclamation is 100% factual, Sis. The primary reason for my skepticism is marked in point by this question: how many times have you deleted your account and taken a step back from social media all together? If it didn't affect you the way you'd like others to believe, would there be a need for a definitive break? I've said it numerous times.

Many will say they don't concern themselves with the opinions and views of others who are watching. The reality, though, is often hidden underneath a defensiveness that fuels that acute "I don't care..." pronouncement. While you may not allow the opinions and views of others to directly sway your actions and thoughts, truth be told, prying eyes (especially during our darkest time) can affect you adversely. In fact, the perceived scrutiny of the world's prying eyes also contribute to reinforcing the negative ideas already brewing inside us – you know, those self-defeating insecurities we all secretly harbor within ourselves that are, in essence, backed up and given validity based on the opinion of outsiders.

It's gotten damn hard to "play" the best you when you really feel like nothing is going right in your life, and yet everyone around you is watching. You know what I say, Sis, LET THEM WATCH! Transparency is liberating as fuck, to a degree. So what if you're not at your best? You never really know who else out there in the world can benefit from your story. I say if they want to watch, make sure that comeback is strong and fully see it through so your struggles may encourage someone else's triumph. This is what I mean when I say there is beauty in all things. I can attest to that in my weakest moments when I yearned for someone who'd been through the valley before me to share their tale of perseverance and inspire me to forge on. For someone else to see the growth after transforming a struggle into a string of successes – even if we count them as small victories – let those who have yearned for guidance know that no struggle is in vain. We see the peaks but we're more inclined to believe the lows of our valleys. Don't worry yourself to much about the naysayers and haters watching. Do it for the queens who stagger behind you as you create a path to a better reality.

I know the ability to be transparent in our lowest times isn't a task for everyone. You know what you can handle, Sis! If you truly feel incapable of fixing yourself in front of the mirrored eyes of the world, then do what makes you most comfortable to maximize your moments of growth. If you don't feel like you can truly heal in real-time under the purview of virtual watchers, please know that it is also OK shut it down and shut them out!

Take some time for you! It's OK to hide yourself away from the world while you work on you. You are like a phoenix rising from the ashes. You will emerge from the simmering rubble of life's inferno by building your faith walk. Take time to write a new vision for yourself. You're the author; now change the narrative.

Our present-day society has become such an immersive experience of viewership and social voyeurism. Every single aspect of everyone's life is generally laid out and played out for the entire world to bear witness. With just a few keystrokes, you can paint whatever image of yourself you'd like for the world to see. You can share as much of yourself and your life as you're comfortable with. It's all at your own discretion. Just be careful of that double edged sword, when seeking instant gratification based on external approval and/or acceptance of others. You can open yourself up to unwanted negatives. While some may see social media as harmless indulgence, I call this a recipe for mental and emotional disaster – if you're not rooted and confident with who and where you are.

Think of all the issues we face in everyday life, coupled with the constant need for society's approval. I am speaking from experience; with these connections via social media, we open ourselves to a whole new level of chaos that feeds upon the fact that so many of us are not grounded in our own truth.

It's been said that we've become more connected as a society than ever before, yet more disconnected from real connections, personal relationships, and tangible experiences at the same time. Speaking for myself, I can recall waking up in the morning and, as soon as I opened my eyes, find myself reaching for my phone. I wasn't checking for missed phone calls or texts; I was instinctively reaching for my phone to log onto social media. Like so many others, I felt the overwhelming need (as the first task of the day) to partake in viewing, dissecting, judging, and measuring what everyone else in the world was doing. From there I'd find myself lying in bed for upwards of an hour, taking inventory of other people's lives.

I'd find myself so entrenched in the happenings of the people on my friends list, or the accounts of random strangers I'd never heard of before, that I found myself more invested in viewing their lives than focusing on my own. It was more than just a habit. It felt as though I'd became an addict to virtual voyeurism. You know what I also noticed about my self-diagnosed social media habit? I'd subjected myself to an overload of hateful opinions, a constant cascade of violent videos, an endless barrage of woe-is-me posts that I'd scroll through daily without fail.

Exposing myself in this way drained me badly and ultimately forced me to a realization that I was no longer okay with that. As a result, I imposed my own protective limits on myself as to how I would indulge in social media. As a business owner, I am inclined to market my products and engage my base via social networking. The protective measures I put in place as a woman, mother and friend do not dictate what I share, with whom I share, and what I take in as the result of other's sharing. I drew a hard line in the sand on my concerns over the "opinions" of others. After all, everyone has an opinion doesn't mean that every opinion is valid. Point taken!

I protect the things I'd like to keep just for me and keep them private. Now I share my stories and welcome the feedback and testimony of others willing to engage in topics of interest to me. I am no longer anchored to social media in the way I was before, taking in all the mess and practically welcoming the mind-altering fuckery of others. Putting these barriers and structures into place in my social media life now allows for an experience that is not as cumbersome and emotionally taxing as before. I've detached from what people think, I am simply indifferent; the criticisms and/or critiques no longer move me in a way that alters how I CHOOSE to feel that day. See, I set my intentions for the day long before I set eyes on the lives of others via social media platforms. This was my way of taking back control. The social devils had their teeth sunk in too deep, creating boundaries and setting my intentions first helped aid me in loosening their grip!

I'd recommend taking a moment, Sis, to examine your social media presence. What do your interactions online look like? How are these interactions feeding you? Importantly, how are these interactions affecting you?

EXERCISE 7.0

How much time do you spend perusing social media sites daily?
_____ Hours per day
_____ Hours per week (daily total multiplied by 7)
_____ Hours per month (weekly total multiplied by 4)
_____ Hours per year (Monthly total divided by 12)

I'm willing to bet that you've calculated a lot of time dedicated to minding the business of others. Am I right?

If you're a business owner/entrepreneur, I'm sure that you dedicate a lot of time towards social media to increase your brand awareness. I get it! In this case, dear, you are exempt from this exercise. However, if you are not using social media as a tool to help grow in your passion and purpose, you may be misusing it, which means you are potentially mismanaging your time and your connections. I can assure you if you're continually misusing these tools of instant connectivity, you are also mismanaging your level of fucks given towards your own mental and emotional wellbeing.

Please, don't be her Sis!

The Myth V. The Reality of the Strong Black Woman

13

Imagine a world where you somehow managed to survive every trial and tribulation encountered on your journey by being steadfast, pushing through, and moving beyond each obstacle with such perceived ease that even you forget your name isn't Superwoman. You somehow managed to come out of times so tumultuous that the thought of it still gives you chills when you sit back and think of how far you've come. (Pause and take a moment to reflect. You feel that feeling? That's called Gratitude, and it is the best medicine for any ill in life).

Yet, also imagine this same world, as far back as you can remember, when you were met with expectations from everyone around you who said, "Even if you feel like breaking, you cannot... you can never fold." These expectations required you to be ON at all times. Tuh! As if you haven't been through enough. Now that superhuman strength you've displayed to the world has somehow become your Achilles heel. See, none of us are totally aware of the so-called expectations bestowed upon us until we're expected to show up, right?

It's as if at birth we somehow were unceremoniously crowned to carry this expectational weight - weight that no one ever asked or even assessed whether we were equipped to handle. Until one day you realize that you've been handed this unimaginable task of carrying said expected baggage. And what do we do? Without the proper tools in place, we don't stop to take the time to assess our own limitations. We move forward, dragging that bag behind us, never setting any boundaries or load capacities. We simply prepare our bags for the long haul on every subsequent journey in life with the weight of those implied expectations weighing us down to the damn ground. And yet, throughout every phase of our lives, we are in line with the daunting task of carrying these bags and trying like hell to keep pace.

We carry them through all our ups and downs and the worst moments endured, through each new reckoning of our shortcomings, each moment counted as a failure and every devastating disappointment we face. We do as many of us are told. We push forward with this baggage weighing on our feminine frames every step of the way. Sounds like an exhaustingly insurmountable task to endure. Well, Sis, this is what it feels like to wear the role of a "strong black woman". As I'm sure you may already know. Day in, and day out.

I'm here to tell you the ideal you have come to know is a myth! Frankly, as black women, we gotta cut the bullshit when it comes to the fictional ideology of who we are and how we should operate on our journey through life. It's time to pick off the dead weight of societal expectations in a fruitless effort to live up to someone else's standard of what your black experience is and should be!

Why would we ever allow others, who have not walked in our shoes or held to the same standard as us, define our stories? Our constant – and often failed attempts to live up to the perpetual myth of the "strong black woman" has contributed to so many ailments within our individual experiences of black womanhood. No one person should bear the burden of being a strong, mythical superhuman creature all the time.

To be honest, it doesn't matter what a person's gender or race is. This is unfair and biased within and of itself - male or female. Certainly, within this particular book, I am more explicitly concerned about my own gender demographic here. Our Brother Malcolm X described the black woman as the most disrespected, unprotected person in America. Did you hear that? He didn't say the most disrespected, unprotected person in a specific city or region. He said in AMERICA.

This country has historically been the biggest detractors of the Black Women's Movement and the biggest betrayer of our plight. To take it one step further, I'd like to add to Brother Malcom's sentiment that we're also among the most incorrectly idealized persons in America.

Look at it this way, if we've already been labeled as the most disrespected and unprotected, why are we STILL willing, at any moment, to throw on the proverbial cape and embody mystical superhuman strength when we are not in sound mental, emotional, physical, or spiritual shape to do so? Now don't get me wrong, it's admirable to be viewed as strong – remember, it's our God-given magic! As many of you know, black women are strong as fuck! Don't believe me? Look around at the woman standing next to you. I guarantee you'll see her scars and her muscles flexing simultaneously. We've been through it all! Many of us prevail as a sheer testament to our strength within. But there is no such thing as being indisputably strong ALL the time, especially coming from the point of ongoing self-sacrifice, which ironically seems to be synonymous with being a black woman.

There was a story in the news recently, regarding a heinous murder-suicide committed by a female doctor who took the life of her two adult children then turned the gun on herself. When I first heard the story, I was immediately drawn to it like a moth to a flame. I gathered as many details as I could from articles, think-pieces, statements of her family and friends, and social media posts surrounding the dates that led up to the devastating event in an attempt to analyze her life from the outside in. The recurring theme I gathered from family, friends, and associates' statements was that no one could fathom how this accomplished doctor, a woman of prominence within metro Atlanta society, who had founded her own business and raised her children with pride, could commit such a crime.

I read over each question that left many wondering, "How could this have happened?" Sadly, the only thing I could conclude was a complete understanding of how such a thing could happen. The answer to the disbelief was as plain as day to me, and the reason is that I knew in my core that I'd be an entire lie if I said I had not entertained the idea of taking my own life.

Yes! At my lowest of low points, I was completely convinced that no one would even miss me, and life would go on as it always does.

However, the reward would mean freeing myself from the pain, guilt, trauma, and loneliness I was enduring on what seemed like an ongoing basis. I, too, can stand here and boldly admit that I had also flirted with the idea of suicide. And there it is! The great reveal, as painful and shameful as it may sound.

I know so many people around me have struggled with these suicidal thoughts, but unfortunately so many will never talk about. I assume the refusal to talk about it is based on the debilitating fear of judgment from those on the outside who we are convinced could never understand our level pain. Mix that with the overwhelming need to protect our images as unbreakable pillars within our culture. How can we address our issues and treat them if we're so afraid to give anyone concrete proof of our weakness by opening up and admitting our mental health challenges. God forbid that a "strong black woman" comes across as weak in today's society, that's oh so taboo.... (insert sarcasm).

I wonder if the doctor who took her own life and the lives of her children felt that same overwhelming sense of hopelessness so many of us have become familiar with from various points turmoil in our respective lives. Was it those same feelings of hopelessness that prevented her from expressing her pain, as many of us do, out of fear of being judged and verbally crucified by our peers? While it would be totally ignorant to speculate because I did not know this woman personally, for some reason I felt completely drawn to her story when the news of her death broke. Something deep in me resonated with this woman. There was something buried within me that connected to her, igniting feelings of pure empathy and compassion.

Oh, how I wish I could have reached out to her, even if only to hear her out or maybe offer her a shoulder to cry on. Sometimes all we need as mythical figures of strength is a safe space to simply BE and deal with judgment. I know there have been many times in my life when I've truly needed that safe space to let lose my emotions. A place where I can just throw my burdens down on the table like a jigsaw puzzle and have enough time to process things and figure it all out.

But when you're expected to always "JPT (just push thru)", you don't get those necessary moments to simply be a human being with will real human issues. A huge attribute of being human is having the ability to FEEL. It is no coincidence that a key component in healing is allowing yourself to FEEL, acknowledging and releasing them. Whatever feelings that arise in you are all a part of your human healing process. If you feel weak, so be it! These are times when you can work through what has broken you down and provide yourself necessary moments to recharge.

It's all a part of the process that many of us miss out on regularly in our efforts to be Superwoman 24/7-365. I'll assume that, like myself, you've had to play your own life coach during times of turmoil. At best, we become our own motivators during those dark experiences. But how many of us know that sometimes the pit of turmoil is so dark and so damn deep that we are easily swallowed whole within an abyss of its pain? We spend countless hours of our day examining every array of our lives. We often further anguish ourselves by repeatedly mulling over moments of the horribly tragic times that make us feel like we have nothing else to live for. Some of us stay in this mental pit much longer than we'd like, holding on, praying steadfastly until we finally experience a small break in our cloud. We stay there until we finally see the smallest glimmer of a silver lining, knowing that our storms will eventually pass and finally allow us to breathe again.

See, we know, Sis, that the sunshine after the storm hits with a different glow. Bouncing back is what we do, as we somehow manage to conjure up enough will and persistence necessary to help pull us out of our most depressing moments. For me, when my spirit is full and I can focus on the beauty in life versus the temporary struggles - if only for a moment - it feels like some of the struggles I have endured were indeed worthwhile. I always say I'd do it all over again if it makes me better! If we can learn to use reverence to allow ourselves to find joy in the peacefully pleasant moments, we'll notice over time that the storms we encounter become lighter and lighter.

I can honestly say that there were many times when I wasn't so sure I'd ever see the light at the end of the tunnel. But through it all, I knew one thing for sure; I was deathly afraid of the stigma that came with appearing weak because I often took on way more than I could handle in my efforts to "Just Push Thru." If only I'd known then that the maintaining all the baggage I decided to carry was not only optional but sorely unfair, I would have dropped that shit a long time ago!

The fact that I was so afraid to be viewed as weak is scary as hell to admit to myself, let alone to anyone reading this. Yet here I am talking about it. Why? Because I know this is a subject we absolutely MUST discuss. So please, look at me. Use me as an example if you'd like. I've always been "that one." You know the one that all my other girlfriends and family members turn to when they're at their wits end, simply needing an ear to vent or a shoulder to cry. Here I am. Open, vulnerable, and willing to admit that I, too, managed to become the reigning president and CEO of the pseudo always-on, always-strong black women club.

My question to you, Sis, is, "Would you also include yourself as part of that same club of phonies?" Not only is it impossible to be strong all the time, but it is grossly unkind to expect that of yourself or anyone else for that matter. Yes, there are times when we are pillars of strength: we're magical, beautiful and all that other good shit. However, we are also very human, which means it's okay to take off your cape! There will be days when you are not the strongest woman in the room- again, it's okay.

EXERCISE 8.0

Write down the exact traits or self-descriptions that makes you feel strong, and the feelings or actions you label as weaknesses.

<u>List your perceived strengths</u>

1. _____
_____

2. _____

3. _____

4. _____

5. _____

List your perceived weaknesses

1. _____

2. _____

3. _____

4. _____

5. _____

The Power of the Twin Necessities 14

As women, we tend to move through this life with all the things we've collected, be it hurt and pain, forgiveness and acceptance or simply our mere desire to succeed. We carry these things around with us like our favorite accessories packed in compact toiletry bags. What I've often noticed is many of us forget to pack two of the most important necessities for overcoming almost any obstacle – the twin necessities that many of us forget as we push forward in our day-to-day. We forget to allow ourselves the beautiful healing power that comes with applying Grace and Gratitude to those trying situations we encounter. Just as sure as you would not leave home without your lip gloss and brow liner, we do ourselves no justice when we step out into this world and forget to pack the 2 G's.

Grace is an amazing thing indeed! The word "Grace," as referenced here, is described as "the love and mercy given to us by God as He desires us to have it, not necessarily because of anything we have done to earn it." Grace is knowing that you are loved regardless of what your immediate surroundings reflect. Grace is knowing that out of loving kindness, you are granted mercy in times of struggle so you may forgive yourself for your missteps. Sis, if you allow yourself a moment of reverence to simply bask in the idea that grace covers you on your walk in life, you'll surely have to marvel in its presence.

Grace simply says that I am ENOUGH in this moment and that I will not feel as if I am anything less than the love I desire. When we go through challenges, it's easy for the ills of this world to collapse in on us like a planned demolition. Life's challenges can level you if you're not grounded and surrounded by the beauty of God's grace. Even if you don't subscribe to a specific religion, I'm sure you know the workings of a higher power when you see one.

Grace is like one of those little trinkets we keep with us until the end of time; we remember its purpose and make it a point to never let a day go by without it. Grant yourself some grace, Sis, and in all your abundance, give grace to those around you. See, most things are cyclical in this life, meaning what you give will surely be returned in some form. Grace is one of the best gifts you can give, and speaking from personal experience, it is one of the best gifts to receive.

Grace alone is a great feeling to possess, but if you really want to increase your circle of abundance, Sis, try pairing the bountiful magnetism of grace with its twin accessory known as the awe-inspiring feeling of Gratitude. Gratitude, as described here, is explained as "being immensely and pleasingly thankful; ready and willing to show appreciation for and to return kindness towards others."

It took me over 30 years to truly understand the hidden power we harness by learning to embody a strong spirit of gratitude. Whatever we encounter, there is always a point in your journey, no matter how tumultuous, where we look to find that silver lining. Even in the darkest of times, there is something you can focus on to help you cultivate a sense of gratitude. Being grateful for the smallest of things amid your biggest struggle will assist you with remaining grounded during times when it's easy to get swept away.

How many times have you been in the eye of a tornado in your life and simply needed something to hold on to, when it seems like everything around you was in complete and utter chaos? I don't know about you, Sis, or what you've lived, but I know what I know, and that is no one is exempt from the struggle. Yet not everyone is aware of how to create their own anchors! Gratitude, for example, says, "Yes, I've lost my job.... but I am able to sustain a roof over my head." Instead of focusing on the lack of employment in this scenario, gratitude is shifting your focus to the positive, recognizable, bright spot in the situation.

I am not one to trivialize the challenges we face in life. I know many of us deal with a much deeper loss than losing a job. However, I also know that no matter the struggle, actively searching for and zeroing in on what we are grateful for keeps us tethered to the belief that not every dark moment lasts forever. Try using grace and gratitude as your lighthouse! If you make it a habit, you, too, can one day pay it forward by giving grace and gratitude to others, further expanding that beacon of light. Spread it around, Sis, let it be contagious!

Now that we know the power and importance of the 2 G's, let's make a vow to put these twin necessities to work in our lives! It took me years to learn that no circumstance, outside of death, is without a way out. Through trial and practice, I learned to use the 2 G's as a weapon to light my way when my trials told me there was no exit. I started practicing meditation daily and implored the ideas of extending grace and gratitude to enter my inner vision. Here is where I found implementing the twin necessities to be most powerful – by taking a moment in the early AM, and even throughout the day as needed, to project these feelings out into the universe.

The level of peace that subsequently followed my meditative practices was priceless. I am asking that you try this as well. Find yourself a quiet space for prayer and meditation. Take a moment of solitude and allow the spirit of gratitude to engulf you as you take mental inventory of everything you've overcome and everything you can count yourself grateful for in the moment. I don't care if you can only find gratitude for having running water. Obviously, you know what it's like to not have something that many of us take for granted. Use it Sis! Use whatever it is you can find – people, places, or things. Meditate on the feeling of immense thankfulness to possess what it is you've been without a time or two in life.

Trust me this works wonders! And guess what? In that moment, you are allowing yourself Grace under fire! Grace is giving yourself a reprieve of mercy by acknowledging where you are and knowing this moment is not forever. I say even if you're not facing any struggles, this is the prime time to practice the 2 G's. What better time to rejoice and give to the universe what we all so desperately need at some point or another as we continue to push upward and onward?

Increasing the power of healing and abundance is not the only reason why we must actively and continuously harness the power of the 2 G's. We need to be armed and ready at all times, primarily in the face of war, keeping them ingrained within us at all times.

Remember that life is cyclic. To embrace and harness grace and gratitude means that you can evoke these same feelings in others if you so make it your mission! Think about it like this: If the idea of abundance creates more abundance in the form of giving and receiving, just think of that feeling of gratitude you'll pass on to others if they actively see you practicing what you preach.

If those in your immediate circle witness you extending a spirit of Grace in moments that are generally trying, just think of the exchange you're offering by leading by example and modeling the embodiment of Grace firsthand. Ask yourself how most of us learn when and where to apply our tools in life? How do we learn to model our behaviors and patterns in our quest for success in life? Typically, we follow by sight. Giving out the 360-degree gift of Grace and Gratitude ensures these elements will return to you full circle. That constant flow creates an unending stream of abundance. As you pour from your cup, they shall surely be poured back into yours!

As we seek, so shall we give; nothing teaches us that better than the continuous practice of exuding the wonderful spirit of the 2 G's! Remember, as sure as you would not go out into the battlefield without your protection of armor, know that the twin necessities, Grace and Gratitude, should always be with you wherever you go. Given freely and received abundantly. There is no other way I can put it! Whatever you do, don't leave home without them!

EXERCISE 9.0

Take a moment to focus on at least 3 things you can find Gratitude for in your life! Write them down. Make them simple and remember to revisit them often. Keep that wave going, Sis, remembering that gratitude creates abundance.

1. _____

2. _____

3. _____

Take a moment to find an area where you can visualize extending the restoring power of Grace to your life. List 3 areas where you can apply the spirit of Grace to your life! Just as I said before, write them down and revisit them often, if not daily!

1. _____

2. _____

3. _____

Life-Unapologetically 15

Let us all collectively *WOOSAH*, inhaling and exhaling with deep healing breaths. As you inhale and exhale, embrace the premise of letting go of all the things in this life that no longer serve you well. Know that it is OK to move forward and upward no matter where you come from or what you've been through. Give yourself the permission to try again, always!

We've tackled some tough items in the previous chapters. I'm sure by now that your heart and mind need to tread on some much lighter territory. If you are indeed still following along with me, first and foremost, much gratitude to you, Queen! Holdfast, we are almost at the finish line! But before we cross over into what I pray is a profound healing and glorious new beginning for all of us, I'd like to take a moment to make sure we touch and agree on how to cultivate and truly LIVE the life we want and desire.

Let's make a pact amongst ourselves to live the life we imagine as unapologetically as possible. The key to cultivating the life you imagine is knowing in your soul that your power is in your healing, and your proof of healing is in how you live going forward. If you can look around you, calling forth that same spirit of Gratitude we just visited in the last chapter and manage to muster up enough fight to

LIVE the best life for you – designed by you – then you, my love, are already on your way.

It's not enough to simply talk it, one must learn to walk it! Charge forward in your life with such a presence that even the clouds will have to stop and bow to take notice. You get where I'm going with this, right? To get the results you desire, you must farm fertile land, for the seeds that you sow have everything they need to grow. That means creating an environment where you not only harvest the seeds sown, but you can also turn around and reinvest the same jewels you've harvested through your struggles with those around you. This is where we observe the fruits of life - by how we live it!

Of course, we all have a particularly important story to tell regarding our personal triumphs and failures. Not just speaking for myself, many of you have witnessed or are currently in the depths of struggle. Be it mental, emotional, or physical low, these moments can induce the burdening feelings of depression, anxiety, and self-doubt within even the strongest of people. However, just as a phoenix rises from the ashes, you've managed to weather life's storms and return bigger, better, stronger, and much wiser than ever before. But for God's Grace! Am I right, Sis?

Surely, if you're fresh out of a stormy season in your life, you're at the point where you'd like to start applying the lessons (or jewels) you've learned on your life's journey. The proper application of these learned lessons will help fortify your effort to forge ahead with clarity in a sound direction, especially if you desire to create a more peaceful and fulfilling existence. I hope that's what you want for yourself, Sis.

If so, know that you are not alone. The desire to do better is generally preceded by a string of chaotic and/or catastrophic events. So, what exactly do we learn from our most trying times? I say the number one lesson is the realization that we only get one shot at this thing called life, so let's try our best to make it the one we choose to live no matter the circumstances surrounding us.

This, in essence, means chucking the proverbial deuces to any and everything in your life that no longer serves you, or better yet, whatever does not aid your growth beyond your current state. When you start to explore what makes you feel fulfilled, you begin creating a blueprint of all the things that contribute to your own happiness and personal fulfillment. Looking at your blueprint, you must then make the commitment that whatever it is, you're going to do it and doing it well!

I heard a quote from an obviously wise man who encourages us all to "pursue your passion with such intent that your only intent will become the need to pursue your passion." If that doesn't make sense, Sis, it means that whatever you see for yourself that brings you a sense of joy, purpose, and profound peace, do that shit! You are the only one who can do what you were put here to do! That's law.

Although it's not written law per se, the premise of spiritual law definitely applies here. You were uniquely created and derived from a higher power. Your gifts were specifically designed to come forth into your life. Honor you gifts in such a way that no outside approval is necessary for you to do what it is you desire to do.

I remember a time in my early to mid-twenties when I kept myself surrounded by an abundance of people. My circle was deep - filled with people I defined as either a friends or close associates. My crew consisted of a variety of people, all on very different paths in their own respective lives. We hung out together regularly, mostly participating in unproductive things, yet we found solace in each other's company, sometimes forging collective bonds in our functional and dysfunctional ways of life.

However, as I grew older and my vision for my own life started to expand, I noticed my circle start to dwindle significantly. Now, as I approach my forties, I can count my true friends and close associates on one hand. Why is that, you may ask. I attribute this shift to becoming clearer in my purpose and ultimately having the courage to walk my own road regardless of others' paths. See, I was determined to do "me" at all costs, something I can honestly say has paid off in the long run.

I could have easily cowered and turned away from my innate desire to expand beyond the constricting confines of my environment. My saving grace was my insatiable desire for growth. This created an absolute need within me to know more, experience more, and take in more than what I'd become limited to in my immediate circle. That desire fueled my fire and helped me to hone the capabilities I needed to create the life I'd envisioned for myself beyond those spaces I'd grown up in.

Sis, it is my testament that anytime you start to feel that need to stretch, that tug in your spirit that encourages you to spread your wings, do not ignore it! The feeling in your spirit urging you to grow may cost you a close friend, some family members, even a relationship partner, but trust me when I say that to move beyond, sometimes you have to leave behind! And watch this, when you begin that slow rise above your past, you may even start to notice that your old friends/associates tell you you're "acting funny" or say things like "Oh, you think you're better than us now."

By the time this starts happening, you won't even have to think too hard about who goes with you to the next level and who gets left behind. Anyone who loves you and has your best intentions at heart will respect your growth, not criticize it. When you finally take time to look around, your circle will undoubtedly become smaller. I'll then pose this question to you: yes, your circle is smaller, but has it become more impactful? If you can honestly look around and answer with an emphatic "yes," you are already on that road to living the life you want by creating circles that foster growth and development and implore you to reach your highest potential!

There's a saying that goes, "you can't soar with the eagles if you're on the ground surrounded by pigeons." Your immediate circle is a direct reflection of where you are in life. If you desire more, bigger, better or anything above your current position, you must make that clear. Write down your vision; make it plain. Keep that desire in the forefront of your mind. I guarantee you, Sis, that you'll start to see an immediate shift in the company you keep. And as I stated, some may have an opinion about how you choose to move once you have chosen your own path, yet you must commit to your path and make no apologies for it! Those who genuinely rock with you will always understand.

Independent decisions are tough at times, Sis! But all in all, they are necessary factors of adulthood. I always say the willingness to make the tough decisions designed to move us forward is what separates adults from children. You are the executor of your estate! No one else will look out for you the way that you do. Besides, no one sees your vision for yourself better than you do. So, who better to make the choices necessary to move the needle forward on your journey? That is your power, and I emphatically implore you to never give that away.

There are times for collective decision making. For instance, in a marriage, relationship, or business partnership. Yet during said collective decisions, don't sit content in your spirit. I urge you to examine 1. The driving force behind the decision, 2. What make you so uncomfortable with what has been agreed upon, and 3. Will said decision yield the best possible return on your investment?

If your answer is no to two or more of these questions, does the collective attachment still suit your journey. I'm not saying get a divorce because you disagree with two or three components. I am saying that it may be time for a healthy reassessment. Let no one make you feel bad or guilty for routinely assessing and reassessing what suits you. Whether it's a life partner, business partner, or friendship, your vision is yours. Own it, protect it, and nurture it accordingly! Never apologize for holding your vision in high regard. Walk kindly and treat everyone fairly with respect and love, yet never allow their guilt to become your burden. We already have enough accumulated baggage in this lifetime, love. The opinions and views of others are not your burden to bear...Sorry NOT sorry.

EXERCISE 10.0

Let's take a moment. I'd like you to reflect on a time when you had to make a hard decision in life i.e., ending a relationship, severing ties with close friends, resigning from an unfulfilling job, and/or leaving a nonproductive business partnership. In hindsight, now that you've made that move, can you honestly look back and see how executing that critical decision was necessary to move forward into more meaningful connections.

I'm talking about, devoid of self-pity and the struggles that ensued from the disconnect, can you now see the clarity you felt in making the decision, and why it had to happen clear your path leading you in a different direction? As you revisit this pertinent experience, take time to detail the situation below (or feel free to write this down in your own separate journal).

_____
_____
_____
_____
_____
_____
_____
_____
_____

Who's Your Connect?

In the previous chapter, we touched on the idea that your immediate circle is a direct reflection of who you are and where you are in your life. Don't believe me, Sis? Then I challenge you to take full inventory of your current circle. If you find that you are frustrated in any areas of your life, i.e., stagnant in your dreams, depressed out of your mind, pessimistic about your future, without a solid plan for achieving goals, or if you lack support or feel unfulfilled in your life's mission, I ask that you truly examine the dichotomy of your immediate relationships.

After your analysis, you may find the relationships you've aligned yourself with are operating on negative frequencies. If this is indeed the case, I say it's time to reboot and refresh your connects!

Once you begin to breakdown and categorize the connections you've managed to build, you must decide which relationships are worth watering by consciously contributing more care, effort, attention and/or focus on those relationships that uplift you and help to propel you forward.

On the other end, it is just as important to also acknowledge the relationships that must be severed at the root, by cutting ties with people and/or things in your life that take away from your growth process. Do me a favor, Sis, and please be honest with yourself here. It would be to your detriment to sugarcoat the truth about your current personal and profession interactions. If you identify the correlation between how these relationships were curated, i.e. what in your life attracted them into your space, then you can properly address and eradicate the issues that continue to foster ongoing negative connections. To make an informed assessment, you must ask yourself: what keeps me tied to individuals or situations that are not working in my favor? What permissions am I giving myself, consciously or subconsciously, that continue to attract negative behaviors into my fold?

Listen, Sis, if you're of a certain age (and I'll assume you are, reading this book), you know there comes a time in our lives when we must end connections that do not positively aid in our growth. Whether it be mentally, emotionally or spiritually, our connections over the age of 30 should help usher in a stage of life that requires focus, goal-mining and cultivation and that expands our current thought processes and challenges any beliefs that no longer serve us.

Your circle should, in essence, contribute to your growth versus constricting your ability to move beyond your current state. It's that simple! Now, I'm not advocating for one-sided relationships where you are only soaking up all of someone else's time, positive energy, and knowledge, giving nothing in return. Rather, I am suggesting that you align yourself with relationships that continuously fill you. It then becomes your duty to pour back into those around you in the same areas of personal growth and positivity. This is how we create a paradigm where our cups are rarely empty.

If you're pouring positivity into someone else, and they're pouring positivity into you, no one's cup is ever empty. Whether it be male or female friendships, a mentorship or romantic relationship, just make sure it's a real connection. I am using the word "real" here subjectively. It is whatever you define something of substance, not imitation or artificial, but wholly genuine in nature. With everything we will ultimately experience on life's journey, it is imperative to surround yourself with people who are genuine champions of your personal wellbeing.

During your self-assessment phase, you should also measure the relational connects that have attracted positive, more impactful relationships, to you as well. If you can already see a shift or change in your circle, then you are on the right track to building a solid network integral to your desire growth.

Have you heard the saying, "your network determines your net worth"? The concept alone deserves careful consideration. Nothing that does not add to your quality of life should be allowed in. We must be diligent gatekeepers of our spaces. When deciding to link your life with someone else's, or combine your goals, dreams and visions with another person or entity, you must be aware of the risk associated with attaching to someone who does not have your greater well-being at heart.

If you are diligent about protecting your personal investments in people, you will notice how the right connections can be leveraged to help you flourish so you can be the conduit for someone coming up behind you. If you're connected to the right energy source, you can equip someone whose energy aligns with yours and be a stable place for them to plug into if need be.

Now that's what I call a Good Connect! Where I'm from, we view our "Connect" as the "Plug" - a direct source to procure something desired that we otherwise may not have the means to secure. If you can reach out and touch those around you in a way that enriches your life as well as theirs, while also pushing yourself closer toward the realization of your vision, you are on the right path, my love. However, if, when you look around you, there is not one solid connection or person within your network to whom you can turn to secure something you'd otherwise have no access to, whether it be a necessary product, a piece of mind, sound advice, a changed perspective, business/career knowledge, or a place of accountability, you're connected to a bad plug, Sis. Carrying yourself above everything that regularly comes forward to destroy you is no easy feat. It's also not for the faint of heart. You must make sure your connections are strong, robust, and more importantly genuine.

Let's examine this from another perspective. If you were hanging over the edge of a skyscraper, fearing for your life and in desperate need of help, would you reach out for a piece of floss dangled over the edge (by someone who obviously does not have the wherewithal to assess or manage the situation and, more importantly, react in a manner that could save your life)? Or would you reach for the thick knotted rope (a man of great strength who is wise enough to gauge the situation and associated risks and make the proper call to provide the help you need)?

If you're of sound mind, Queen, I think we know the answer to this question. You'd go for the rope you know has a greater chance of ushering you safely to solid ground. This is exactly what your relational connections should reflect! If you plan on going somewhere above and beyond where you are now, you must choose your connects as if your life and livelihood depend on it. Misalignment has proved to be one our greatest hindrances. Often we don't see it until it is too late. Usually, by that time we've dug ourselves into a hole that will take everything we have left to free ourselves from.

I don't know about you, Sis, but I've taken enough L's. If I've learned nothing, it is that not everyone deserves a seat at your table. No matter how nice, sweet, fine, or good in bed a person may be, you must always ask yourself, "How do we fit into the equation of each other's lives that would provide the greatest yield for us both?"

Despite the number of years you've known a particular friend or invested into a business partnership, if the connection does not yield the results you require for your standard of achievement, it is your duty to sever the cords. No love lost; this is where intent meets action, and actions tell the world who we are.

To be completely honest, it is only now as a woman preparing to gracefully enter her 40's that I understand the distinction and impact of my connections. I have some long-standing friendships that have weathered the test of time, which I attribute to our individual commitments to grow in our respective journeys; yet we still find a way to pour into each other with the knowledge we've gathered.

I have mentorships with individuals I've met along my career path who have pushed me to be the best version of myself in the corporate world by imparting their wisdom and career lessons . These people have encouraged me, providing support and information to help me on my quest to fulfill my passion of becoming my own brand. Although these relationships vary, I consider them REAL, solid connects.

It is the desire of these individuals to see me succeed in life. Knowing where I wanted to go was half the battle. Finding the right network of people to get me there proved to be invaluable. As I've worked to cultivate my life with purpose and precision, I've found that these individuals are not short on love, compassion, understanding, care or empathy.

So, let's be clear. Not only did I find allyships, but I also found genuine hearts who shared my desire to actualize my personal vision. I understand this might not be ideal for many, such as those who maylean toward moreso free-flowing connections with others. However, I believe it is important for us, as women, to be intentional in our relationships. This goes for the relationships we allow to engage us as well as the relationships in which we engage.

The importance of aligning yourself with those who support you in your endeavors, the individuals concerned about your plans and your intended method to achieve them, is evident in your current level of progress. I cannot begin to stress how critical this is, Sis. Think about it for a second. How much BS do we encounter in our daily lives? Whether you're attempting to fight your way to the top of the ladder in corporate America, are pursuing the path of entrepreneurship, or planning to settle down, get married and start a family, there are already so many built-in challenges on the path of life.

Where do you possibly have the time or mental capacity to engage in connections that hinder you along the way? You don't need someone around you constantly telling you what you can't do. Specifically, in romantic connections, you don't need to invest time in people who refuse to see and acknowledge your worth as a life partner.

Stop giving your valuable energy to someone who'd rather have you as a life-long baby mama than walk with you as a partner on the road to marriage by honoring your vision of building a solid family structure if that's what you so desire. Nobody has the time or space for that, Sis!

An older Queen once told me, "Feed yourself the food that grows you." Curate real experiences with real connections that consist of substance and are built on love, respect, and truth. When you're running low on fumes, who's there to refuel your tank? As you probably already know, Sis, our strength is sacred and crucial; and dare I say, it is fragile at times. To operate at your highest and fullest capacity, a shift is required to build connections around you that provide consistent replenishment.

These watering holes aid us in our quest to move successfully through life. Why, then, would we not make sure that our energy is thoroughly protected? I am telling you that your connections are your source. Protect the energy that flows through and around you at all times.

Remember, there will come a point where newly aligned, more positive connections will replace the ones you've gotten rid of. Simply because your mindset has changed and you have a desire for connections that will grow you, the universe will abide in compliance. *Let it build, Sis, Let it build!*

Queen, where you are at this very moment and the people who surround you were all once a vision in your mind. It is through your internal desires that the universe gave birth to your vision. Use that same methodology and apply it to your future connections as you continue on your own personal journey to *GREATNESS*. What you see for yourself inwardly should reflect in your outward surroundings.

Are you tied to kites that will help you soar or anchored to weights that hold you down? Whether it be friends, family, colleagues or lovers – all these are vital exchanges of energy moving in and out of your circumference. Be intentional and strategic about where you plug in!

The New Black Woman's Creed

I AM my only hindrance.

I AM my only competition.

I AM only as productive as those I choose to align myself with.

MY vision is only as clear as my plan.

MY plan is only as strong as my own refusal to fail.

MY path is the one that I have consciously chosen with love and insight.

My walk is a testament to sheer perseverance and a reminder that anything is possible.

My belief in myself is my superpower, a true reflection of MY own inner God.

I Promise to Never give up.

I Stand firmly in my truth.

I never bow down.

I rise beyond any trial that comes my way.

I have survived every single thorn placed in my crown.

I wear it proudly.

As the masses look on and the heavens resound,

I vow to change the narrative for every young woman who touches ground as she navigates around the same roads walking swiftly and intently behind me.

Now take what you've learned and run with it!

Peace and love always, E

Made in the USA
Middletown, DE
13 June 2023

32555371R00071